Making Vintage Aircraft in Wood

Joe B. Hicks

 Sterling Publishing Co., Inc.   New York

Dedication

To Michael, my oldest son, whose strength
and maturity is a joy to his mother and me.
Michael, choose the path that you must take
and walk that path straight with your eyes
always upon your Master.

Edited by

Rodman Pilgrim Neumann

Library of Congress Cataloging-in-Publication Data

Hicks, Joe B.
    Making vintage aircraft in wood / Joe B. Hicks.
        p.   cm.
    Includes index.
    1. Airplanes—Models.   2. Airplanes, Military—Models.   I. Title.
  TL770.H54   1990
  629.133′1343—dc20   90-36683
                                                      CIP

10 9 8 7 6 5 4 3 2

© 1990 by Joe B. Hicks
Published by Sterling Publishing Company, Inc.
387 Park Avenue South, New York, N.Y. 10016
Distributed in Canada by Sterling Publishing
℅ Canadian Manda Group, P.O. Box 920, Station U
Toronto, Ontario, Canada M8Z 5P9
Distributed in Great Britain and Europe by Cassell PLC
Villiers House, 41/47 Strand, London WC2N 5JE, England
Distributed in Australia by Capricorn Ltd.
P.O. Box 665, Land Cove, NSW 2066
Manufactured in the United States of America

Sterling ISBN 0-8069-7212-2 Paper

Contents

Color section follows page 64

Introduction

From the beginning of time, man has fantasized of soaring with the eagles. Beholding these majestic creatures with fascination and envy, he has watched as they wing effortlessly through the clouds, higher and higher in the heavens, with only the mysterious wind, as though it were the hand of their Creator, supporting them with grace. Man has freed his imagination to carry him away on wings such as these. He has been with these birds of the heavens, sharing in their magnificence, free from the bonds of earth. He has glided over snow-capped peaks of great mountains, discovering their majesty, and sailed above the deepest seas, reflecting on their mystery. The human race has used this power of fantasy to experience—vicariously—the thrill and freedom of flight for thousands of years.

For the longest of times, the natural laws of the universe were binding on human society, making these fantasies only dreams in which the mind could indulge as the feet stayed firmly on the ground. These dreams, however, were always held close to the heart of this earthbound creature. To be a creature of flight has long been part of man's being, for he has already experienced the freedom, if only in his imagination. It is, perhaps, human nature that once the joy of an experience is known or merely glimpsed—even in dreams—man will not let go of the remotest

possibility of it's becoming reality. He has come to understand that the distance that separates fantasy from reality is often not so great as it seems. By merging that same imagination with an increasingly clever creativity, he has learned to make such dreams possible.

On the morning of December 17, 1903 all of these dreams—of soaring with the eagles—culminated and were fulfilled by a single event. In the United States at a place known as Kitty Hawk, North Carolina, two brothers flew a crude and fragile machine for a time of eleven seconds and a distance of one-hundred twenty feet. This flight of the Wright brothers, however, was not the finish, but only the beginning.

As humankind learned that it really could live out the dream—of soaring with the eagles—the very terms of everyday life changed, as well as the course of history. The reality of flight brought far away places closer. It made the mountains not so high and the seas not so wide. It put freedom in the minds of some and struck terror in the hearts of others. Aviation transformed the modes of travel, as well as the tactics of warfare. And among his achievements man learned to fly both higher and faster than eagles. He has his dream—his wings—now, and he uses them to fly to the far reaches of the earth.

In the pages that follow you have the opportunity to join with those who have flown and many more who only dreamed of flight. You can go to Kitty Hawk, North Carolina, or to a grassy meadow in France, and experience the thrill of escaping the earth, or experience the pleasure of returning to it by landing on the great waters of the Pacific Ocean. You can also go to places such as Pearl Harbor where the experience of flight is not all wonderful. You will see the strengths and power of some of these superb flying machines and yet the delicate fragility of others.

As a woodworker, you already understand the relation of imagination and creativity. Therefore I offer you the challenge to give free rein to your imagination and allow yourself to become like those who have gone before—dream of soaring with the eagles.

As you recreate, in miniature, one-by-one, each of these highly regarded machines, allow your imagination to take you to the places where their reputations were made—over continents or seas, in a particular sky. Allow your senses to become alive to the elements; feel the salt spray as the great flying boats prepare for flight. Experience the then still fresh excitement of combat as aviation finds its role in World War I. Put yourself into the cockpit of an early carrier-based dive-bomber as it begins its dive on enemy ships. Be in command of one of the giant fortresses, a B-17 bomber, high above enemy territory as it delivers its payload.

The following projects will make wonderful display pieces. They can be displayed separately or in relation to other room decor such as memorabilia, including photos, desk or wall plaques, or shadow boxes. A particularly satisfying form of display is to incorporate the piece into the base of a table lamp. Some of these forms of display are illustrated in the pages that follow. Use your imagination to come up with ways of displaying your work that better suit your tastes.

Each set of project instructions is preceded by a list of materials needed for completion. A cutting list is also provided that assigns a reference number for each of the parts needed and indicates the quantity of each part that should be made. These projects can be easily done with the tools most commonly found in a reasonably equipped home workshop. Detailed instructions, supported with accurate scale drawings and step-by-step photo illustrations, have been written to give you a clear understanding of how to go about the construction and assembly process. The actual size of each project is too large for reproduction in this book at full size; the plans have been carefully drawn to show exact shapes and dimensions, and then they have been reduced and superimposed on scale grids. To enlarge these drawings to the full size of the project, use 1″ grid paper. Redraw a portion of the pattern at full size, one square at a time: make the line that will run through your 1″ grid correspond exactly to the line running through the book's smaller square.

It is my hope that you will enjoy yourself building each of these vintage flying machines. In turn I anticipate that with enough time and care you will be pleased with the completed pieces; proud to display them in your home or to present them as gifts to friends and family. Your imagination and creativity will make each one a creation unique to your hand; your craftsmanship will come through as an expression of your talents.

—Joe B. Hicks

·1·
<u>LIGHTER THAN AIR</u>

L'Entreprenant

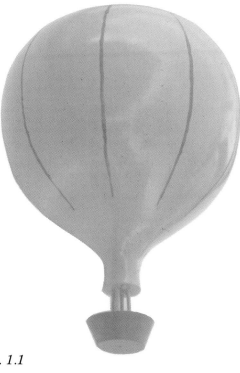

Illus. 1.1

Materials List

Hardwood Block, 5½″ × 5½″ × 8″ ... 1 each*
Hardwood Stock, ¾″ × 2″ × 2″ ...... 1 each
Hardwood Dowel, ⅛″ diameter .... 6″
Carpenter's Glue .... small container

* This hardwood block can be fabricated by laminating seven pieces of ¾″ stock into one unit.

Cutting List

Part 1 ... Balloon .... Make 1
Part 2 ... Gondola .... Make 1

Man began his adventure aloft as early as the eighteenth century by using the physical properties of warm air. Once aware that warmer air rises above cooler air, he thus created what we now know as the "hot air balloon." The *L'Entreprenant* (Illus. 1.1) was flown by the French military for observational purposes in 1794.

Instructions

LAYOUT

1. The balloon (Part 1) is best shaped by turning on a lathe. Prepare a lathe template by tracing the shape of this part (Illus. 1.2) onto a piece of construction paper or thin cardboard. Draw a line down the middle, top to bottom, and cut in half along this line. Now cut out and discard each of the inside half shapes remaining. Retain each outside piece to use as a template to gauge the shape of the part as you turn it on the lathe.

2. Position the hardwood block properly in your lathe and turn out Part 1. Ensure the accuracy of the shape by using the template.

3. After the shape is formed, use various grades of sandpaper to sand it to a smooth finish (Illus. 1.3).

4. Lay out a 1½″ circle on a piece of ¾″ stock for the gondola (Part 1, Illus. 1.2).

5. Using a 1″ drill in your drill press, drill out the middle of this circle to a depth of ¼″. This will be the inside of the gondola (Illus. 1.2).

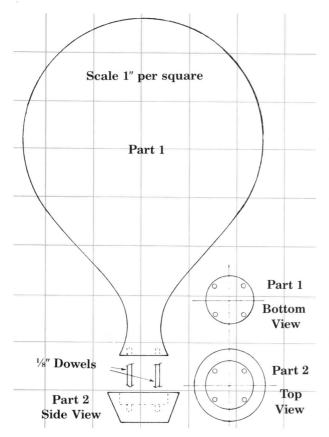

Scale 1″ per square

Part 1

Part 1
Bottom View

⅛″ Dowels

Part 2
Top View

Part 2
Side View

Illus. 1.2   Layout of parts. L'Entreprenant.

Illus. 1.3   Sand each part to a smooth finish suitable for painting.

6. Set your band saw to cut a 20° angle.
7. Cut out the circle on the band saw. The angled cut will create the truncated cone shape desired for the gondola (Illus. 1.3).
8. Sand each of these parts to a finish suitable for painting.

ASSEMBLY

9. Mark and center punch each of the ⅛″ holes at the bottom of Part 1 and also inside the 1″ counterset of Part 2 as shown in Illus. 1.2.
10. Use a ⅛″ drill bit in a drill press to drill each of the holes marked to a depth of approximately ³⁄₁₆″.
11. Cut four sections of ⅛″ dowel to a length of 1¼″. Sand the ends of each so that they insert easily into the ⅛″ holes of each part.
12. Now, glue the dowel sections into the holes at the bottom of Part 1. Be careful to insert them completely into the holes and so that they extend to equal lengths.
13. Place a small drop of glue on the end of each of the extending dowels and position the gondola (Part 2) in place, inserting the dowels into the corresponding holes. Make sure that the gondola is level with the bottom of the balloon before the glue has time to set.
14. The *L'Entreprenant* balloon is now ready to finish. It may be painted to give a more authentic appearance or varnished to show the quality of the material and your workmanship.

·2·
FIRST WINGS OF AVIATION

Wright Flyer

Illus. 2.1

The *Wright Flyer*, sometimes referred to as the "Kitty Hawk," was the first heavier-than-air aircraft to be successfully flown (Illus. 2.1). This flight was made on December 17, 1903 at Kitty Hawk, North Carolina. It was a short flight lasting only eleven seconds and covering a distance of one hundred twenty feet. Nevertheless, it was a successful flight and marks the beginning of the age of aviation that we know today.

Materials List
Hardwood Stock, ¾" × 4" × 15" ......1 each
Hardwood Dowel, ⅜" diameter ....2"
Hardwood Dowel, ¼" diameter ....10"
Hardwood Dowel, ⅛" diameter ....60"
Carpenter's Glue .... small container

Cutting List
Part 1 ... Wing .... Make 2
Part 2 ... Elevator .... Make 2
Part 3 ... Rudder .... Make 2
Part 4 ... Skid .... Make 2
Part 5 ... Propeller .... Make 2
Part 6 ... Engine Half .... Make 1
Part 7 ... Engine Half .... Make 1
Part 8 ... Pully .... Make 1

Instructions

LAYOUT

1. Lay out Parts 1, 2, 3, 4, and 6 on the ¾" stock material (Illus. 2.2). These parts do not require the full thickness of the stock material; where two identical parts are indicated, you can lay out one part, cut to shape, and then rip the two thinner parts from the one thicker one.

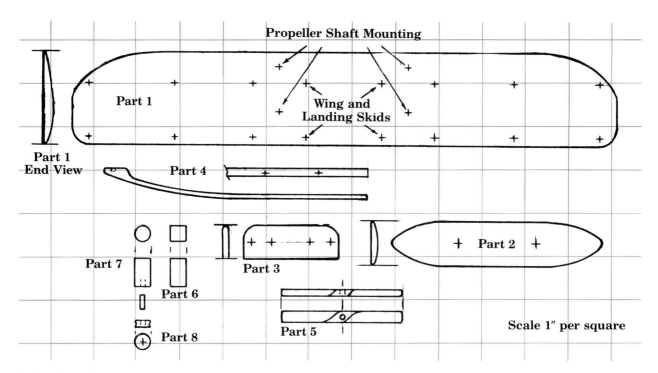

Propeller Shaft Mounting

Part 1

Wing and
Landing Skids

Part 1
End View

Part 4

Part 7

Part 3

Part 2

Part 6

Part 8

Part 5

Scale 1″ per square

Illus. 2.2   Layout of parts. Wright Flyer.

2. Use a band saw to cut these parts to shape (Illus. 2.3).

3. Make Parts 7 and 8 from ⅜″ dowel (Illus. 2.2). Part 8 is the drive pully for the two propellers. Its shape can be made to look more realistic by making a radial cut or groove with a back saw or with a three-corner file before cutting it from the dowel.

4. Make Part 5 from ¼″ dowel (Illus. 2.2). Part 5 is a propeller. First cut it to length, then drill a ⅛″ hole directly through the middle. Insert a ⅛″ dowel section into the hole and use the thinner dowel as a handle as you sand the propeller to shape on a bench-mounted belt sander. Later the hole will be used for mounting the propeller to the finished project. To achieve the propeller shape work on one half at a time; place one half of the ¼″ dowel on the sanding belt with the ⅛″ dowel handle at about a 60° angle to the belt. Work this portion over the sander to create a flat side on the dowel. Try to taper this flat area towards the end so that the middle of

Illus. 2.3   Cut the parts to shape with a band saw. The dowels are cut as you prepare for assembly.

the propeller will retain most of its original thickness for strength. Once you have completed one half of the side, simply turn the part over and in a similar fashion flatten the other side of the same end to create the blade shape. Then repeat the process for the other end of the ¼″ dowel. This may sound a little tricky at first but with a little practice it really is not difficult at all. After the basic propeller shape

Illus. 2.4 Assembly and parts location details for the Wright Flyer.

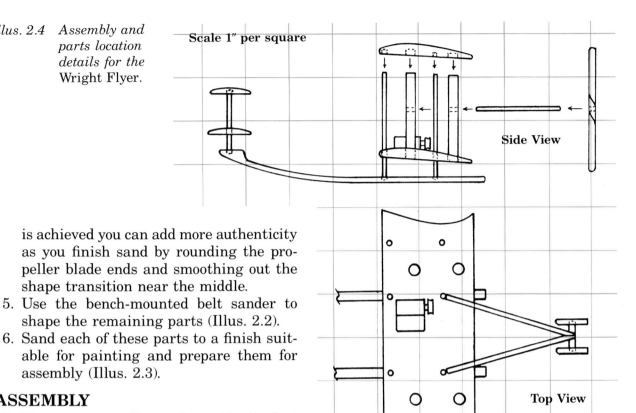

Scale 1″ per square

Side View

Top View

is achieved you can add more authenticity as you finish sand by rounding the propeller blade ends and smoothing out the shape transition near the middle.

5. Use the bench-mounted belt sander to shape the remaining parts (Illus. 2.2).

6. Sand each of these parts to a finish suitable for painting and prepare them for assembly (Illus. 2.3).

ASSEMBLY

7. The two wings (Parts 1) are identical at this time. Choose and mark one to be used as the top wing and the other as the bottom wing.

8. Mark all of the drilling points on the underside of the top wing (Illus. 2.2). These holes will not be drilled completely through the wing but only to a depth of about $3/32''$. Make the hole depth as uniform as possible. All holes are $1/8''$ diameter except the four holes marked for the propeller shaft mounting struts that are to be $1/4''$ diameter (Illus. 2.4).

9. Drill all of these holes in the underside of the top wing at this time.

10. Mark in a similar way the drilling points on the upper surface of the bottom wing. This time drill all of the holes completely through the wing (Illus. 2.2 and 2.4).

11. Now cut twelve sections of $1/8''$ dowel to a length of 2″. These will be the wing struts that actually hold the wings together.

12. Also cut four sections of $1/4''$ dowel to a 2″ length for the propeller shaft mounting struts.

13. Drill a $5/32''$ hole through the middle of each of these $1/4''$ dowel sections. These holes will later be used to mount the propeller shafts (Illus. 2.4).

14. Now place the bottom wing flat on your work bench right side up. You are about to glue the struts into the holes, so you may want to place a piece of waxed paper under your work to prevent it from sticking to the work bench.

15. Glue each of the four propeller shaft mounting struts into the four holes provided. Be sure to align the $5/32''$ holes in the middle of each strut so that they are perpendicular to the wing. This can be done easily by inserting a $1/8''$ dowel section into the holes and gently turning the strut. Also carefully orient the propeller shaft mounting struts so that they are vertical to the work bench.

16. Now glue the twelve wing struts into the twelve outermost ⅛″ holes in the wing—six towards either end of the wing. Work from the middle of the wing outward and make sure they are set vertical to the work bench as shown in Illus. 2.5 (which also shows the four wing and landing skid struts that will be added following the next step).

17. Now glue the top wing in place by inserting all of the existing struts into the corresponding holes in the underside of the top wing. Be sure all of the struts and both wings are properly aligned.

18. Cut the wing and landing skid struts at this time. The two forward struts are 2⅝″ long and the two aft struts are 2⅜″.

19. Using a ⁵⁄₃₂″ drill, slightly enlarge the four holes remaining in the bottom wing. This will make the installation of these struts a little easier.

20. Glue the four wing and landing skid struts in place, being careful to place the longer struts into the forward holes.

21. Mark the three ⅛″ holes in each of the landing skids (Parts 4). Drill these holes to a depth of ³⁄₃₂″ (Illus. 2.2 and 2.4).

22. Glue the landing skids into place on the extending portion of the four wing and landing skid struts. Align the skids so that they are parallel and level with one another (Illus. 2.4).

23. The two elevators (Parts 2) are identical at this time just as the wings had been. Again, choose and mark one for top and one for bottom.

24. Mark the drilling points on the underside of the top elevator and on the upper surface of the bottom elevator (Illus. 2.2).

25. Drill ⅛″ holes to a depth ³⁄₃₂″ into the underside of the top elevator.

26. Drill ⁵⁄₃₂″ holes completely through the bottom elevator.

27. Cut two elevator mounting struts from ⅛″ dowel to a length of 1½″.

28. Glue these struts into the holes in the underside of the top elevator.

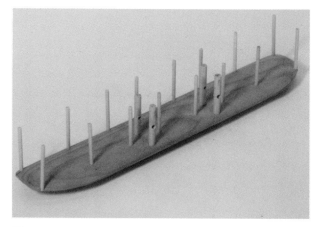

Illus. 2.5 Carefully align all of the struts vertically.

29. Glue the bottom elevator in place by sliding it onto the mounting struts to a point ⅞″ from the top elevator (Illus. 2.4). Be sure that the elevators and the struts are parallel before the glue has time to set.

30. Now glue the elevator assembly into place by inserting the extending portions of the struts into the ⅛″ holes in the forward end of the landing skids. Align so that the struts are parallel with the struts in the wing assembly (Illus. 2.6).

31. Mark the drilling points on the two rudders (Parts 3) as shown in Illus. 2.2.

32. Drill ⅛″ holes to a depth of ³⁄₃₂″ at each of the marked locations (Illus. 2.2 and 2.4).

33. Cut four ⅛″ dowel sections to a length of ⅞″. These will be rudder spacing struts.

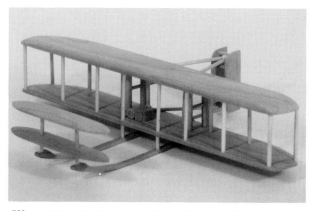

Illus. 2.6 Fully assembled Wright Flyer.

34. Glue these four dowel sections into the ⅛″ holes on one of the rudders. Then position the other rudder over the extending dowels and glue in place. Be sure that both rudders and the four spacing struts are well aligned before the glue sets.

35. Cut four ⅛″ dowel sections to 3″ lengths for use as the rudder assembly mounting struts.

    NOTE: Read through the next two steps and do a dry run: they must be done in one operation to ensure proper alignment during the rudder installation.

36. Glue the rudder assembly mounting struts in place in the following manner. Refer to the top view in Illus. 2.4. The lower set of rudder assembly mounting struts are placed on the upper surface of the bottom wing and butted against the aft wing and landing skid struts. The extending portions of the two struts are adjusted so that they come together at a point. This point must be precisely positioned along the middle line of the elevator-landing skid-wing assembly. The upper set is glued to the underside of the top wing and similarly butted against the aft wing and landing skid struts. The extending portions again converge to a point.

37. Glue the rudder assembly in place by positioning the upper and lower rudder spacing struts on top of the converging ends of the upper and lower rudder assembly mounting struts, respectively. The rudder assembly should be carefully positioned along the middle line to align with the rest of the project. The base of the rudders should clear the work bench by approximately ¼″ when the aircraft is placed on its landing skids.

38. Cut two propeller shafts each 1¾″ long from ⅛″ dowel.

39. Glue the propeller shafts in place by inserting them completely through the holes in the propeller shaft mounting struts until the ends are flush with the forward side of the front mounting strut (Illus. 2.4, side view).

40. Place the propellers (Parts 5) onto the extending sections of the propeller shafts and secure with a drop of glue (Illus. 2.4, side view).

41. Drill a ⅛″ hole through the middle of the propeller drive pulley (Part 8). Also drill into the middle of one end of the cylindrical engine half (Part 7) to a depth of about ⅛″ using the ⅛″ drill.

42. Assemble Parts 7 and 8 by inserting a short piece of ⅛″ dowel, approximately ⅜″ long. Leave about ⅛″ of space between these parts (Illus. 2.2 and 2.4). Glue this assembly together.

43. Glue the rectangular engine half (Part 6) to the partial engine assembly. Align Part 6 with Part 7 as indicated in Illus. 2.2 and 2.4.

44. Refer to Illus. 2.4 to position the completed engine assembly on the upper surface of the bottom wing towards the forward edge and near the right forward landing skid strut. Align carefully, as shown, and secure with glue.

45. Your *Wright Flyer (Kitty Hawk)* is now complete except for painting (Illus. 2.6). The authentic color scheme is fairly simple. All of the flying surfaces—wings, elevators, and rudders—are canvas color. The struts and landing skids are medium brown. The engine assembly is black, and the propellers are light oak stain and clear varnish. If you'd rather show off the wood and quality of workmanship, the entire project will look very nice when done completely with a clear finish rather than painted.

46. To display the finished piece you may prefer simply placing it on a desk or table freestanding as is or possibly on a walnut stand or other fine hardwood base that has a nicely shaped and routered edge and a fine oil finish. A small brass plaque with the name of the aircraft is also an elegant touch.

EARLY WORLD WAR I YEARS

Avro 504

Illus. 3.1

The *Avro 504* was a British-built flight trainer used in the early days of flying (Illus. 3.1). Its use spanned the World War I era. As with many early aircraft it was built primarily of wood and canvas to keep the weight to a minimum.

Materials List

Hardwood Block, 1½" × 1½" × 10" . . . 1 each
Hardwood Stock, ¾" × 4" × 15" . . . . . . 1 each
Hardwood Dowel, ⅜" diameter . . . . 5"
Hardwood Dowel, ⅛" diameter . . . . 50"
Hardwood Toy Wheels, ¾" diameter . . . 2 each
Carpenter's Glue . . . . small container

Cutting List

Part 1 . . . Fuselage . . . . Make 1
Part 2 . . . Lower Wing . . . . Make 1
Part 3 . . . Upper Wing . . . . Make 1
Part 4 . . . Horizontal Stabilizer Half Make 2
Part 5 . . . Vertical Stabilizer . . . . Make 1
Part 6 . . . Propeller . . . . Make 1
Part 7 . . . Landing Skid . . . . Make 1
Part 8 . . . Shock Absorber . . . . Make 2

Instructions
LAYOUT

1. Lay out the fuselage (Part 1) on the hardwood block (Illus. 3.2).
2. Lay out the wings, tail parts, and landing skid (Parts 2, 3, 4, 5, and 7) on the ¾" hardwood stock (Illus. 3.2 and 3.3). These parts do not require the full thickness of the stock material; where two identical parts are indicated, you can lay out one part, cut to shape, and then rip the two thinner parts from the thicker one.
3. The propeller (Part 6) and the two shock absorbers (Parts 8) are made from ⅜" hardwood dowel (Illus. 3.2). Refer to Step 4 of the preceding project for directions on building a propeller (Chapter 2, p. 10).

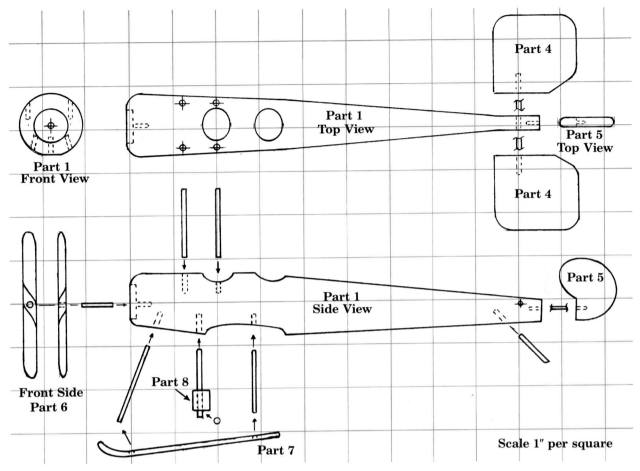

Illus. 3.2   Layout of the fuselage and related parts. Avro 504.

4. Cut all of the above parts to shape with a band saw.

5. Use a bench-mounted belt sander to shape the parts according to Illus. 3.2 and 3.3 and as shown in Illus. 3.4.

ASSEMBLY

6. Mark all of the drilling points on the fuselage (Part 1), each of the wings (Parts 2 and 3), and the tail parts (Parts 4 and 5) as indicated in Illus. 3.2 and 3.3.
NOTE: Some of these holes are to be drilled only partially through the parts. The upper wing (Part 3) is only to be drilled in the underside, and the lower wing (Part 2) is to be drilled from the top side.

7. Use a $5/32''$ drill bit to drill each of these holes as indicated (Illus. 3.2 and 3.3).

8. Use a $7/8''$ center-bore drill to counter set the engine area in the nose of the fuselage (Part 1). Make this counter set about $1/8''$ in depth (Illus. 3.2).

9. Position the lower wing (Part 2) in place in the notch provided in the bottom of the fuselage (Part 1). Ensure that the fuselage is right in the middle of the wing and that the wing and fuselage are properly aligned. Now secure the assembly with carpenter's glue and one or two $3/4''$ brads.

10. Cut four sections of $1/8''$ dowel to $1\frac{1}{2}''$ lengths. These are to be used as the upper wing-to-fuselage mounting struts as shown in Illus. 3.2.

11. Place the upper wing (Part 3) upside down on the work bench and glue these four dowel sections into the four holes

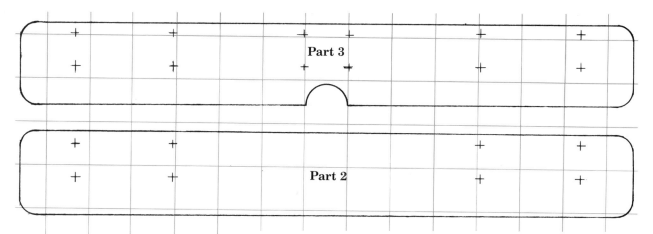

Part 3

Part 2

Scale 1″ per square

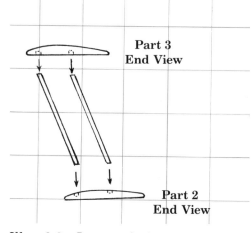

Part 3
End View

Part 2
End View

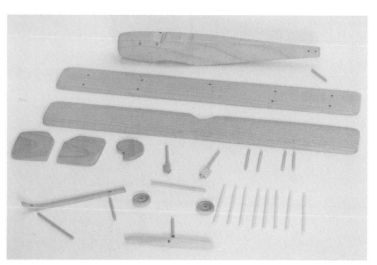

Illus. 3.3   Layout of wings.
Avro 504.

*Illus. 3.4   Cut the parts to shape with a band saw, and
sand each part to prepare for assembly.*

that are near the middle of the wing. Set each dowel perpendicular to the wing.

12. Place the upper wing assembly above the fuselage (Part 1) and insert the four struts into the holes provided. Position the upper wing parallel with the lower wing and in proper alignment with the fuselage. The upper wing should be 1″ above the fuselage. Secure in place with carpenter's glue.

13. Cut eight sections of ⅛″ dowel for wing-to-wing support struts. These dowels should be cut to 2⁷⁄₁₆″ lengths but each may have to be adjusted slightly to the specific layout and variation of dimensions of your wing–fuselage assembly.

14. Glue each of the wing-to-wing support struts into place by placing the ends at— not in—the remaining holes in the wings. These struts tilt forward by about 20° so they are not actually inserted into the holes (Illus. 3.3, end view).

15. Cut two ⅛″ dowel sections to a length of 2″ for the main landing gear struts as shown in Illus. 3.2.

16. Glue these dowel sections into the two holes provided for the main landing gear (Illus. 3.2) to which the two shock absorbers (Parts 8) will be attached. Make sure that they are inserted to the same depth so that the aircraft will sit level when completed.

17. Slide the two shock absorbers (Parts 8) in place by pushing them onto the main landing gear struts until ⅛″ of each strut extends through the bottom of each shock. This will provide a notch for positioning the landing gear axle.

18. The landing gear axle should be a ⅛″ dowel section 2⅜″ long. Glue the axle into the notch mentioned in Step 17 above, so that it extends beyond the main landing gear struts and shocks equally on each side, approximately ⅛″ (Illus. 3.2).

19. Make the landing skid struts with ⅛″ dowel. The forward strut is 2″ long, and the aft strut is 1¼″ long (Illus. 3.2).

20. Install the landing skid struts and the landing skid (Part 7) in one operation to guarantee the best alignment. Position these parts and secure with glue as shown in Illus. 3.5.

21. Position the horizontal stabilizer (Parts 4) in place using a guide pin made from ⅛″ dowel. Be sure to align these parts so that they are level with the wings (Illus. 3.2). Secure with glue.

22. Install the vertical stabilizer (Part 5) with carpenter's glue as shown in Illus. 3.2. Again use a ⅛″ dowel guide pin.

23. Install a short section of ⅛″ dowel for a tail skid as indicated in Illus. 3.2.

Illus. 3.5   Install the landing skid with its struts in one operation to ensure proper alignment.

24. Glue the propeller (Part 6) in place as shown (Illus. 3.2).

25. Install the two ¾″ diameter hardwood toy wheels onto the landing gear axles with a drop of glue.

26. Your *Avro 504* is now complete and ready for finishing (Illus. 3.6). You can either paint the aircraft with authentic colors or varnish the piece to show the wood and quality of your workmanship.

27. This model can be displayed by setting on its own supports or by mounting on a desk plaque. A small brass name plate adds to the quality of the display.

Illus. 3.6   Fully assembled Avro 502.

Handley Page 0/400

Illus. 4.1

The *Handley Page 0/400* bomber was one of the first large multiengine aeroplanes (Illus. 4.1). It was built in 1914 as an effort by the British to combat the German assault. It became an effective weapon as a bomber and had gunners mounted in the nose and amidships to ward off enemy fighter planes.

Materials List

Hardwood Stock, ¾″ × 4″ × 20″ ...... 1 each
Hardwood Dowel, ¼″ diameter .... 10″
Hardwood Dowel, ⅛″ diameter .... 40″
Hardwood Dowel, ¹⁄₁₆″ diameter .... 6″
Hardwood Toy Wheels, ¾″ diameter ... 4 each
Carpenter's Glue .... small container

Cutting List

Part 1 ... Fuselage .... Make 1
Part 2 ... Lower Wing .... Make 1
Part 3 ... Upper Wing .... Make 1
Part 4 ... Horizontal Stabilizer ...... Make 2
Part 5 ... Middle Vertical Stabilizer .. Make 1
Part 6 ... Outboard Vertical Stabilizer Make 2
Part 7 ... Engine .... Make 2
Part 8 ... Propeller .... Make 2

Instructions

LAYOUT

1. Lay out Parts 1, 2, 3, 4, 5, 6, 7, and 8 on ¾″ hardwood stock (Illus. 4.2 and 4.3). Many of these parts do not require the full ¾″ thickness; they must be ripped to the correct thickness.
2. Use a band saw to cut each part to shape.
3. Sand all of these parts to the proper shapes with a bench-mounted belt sander to prepare them for assembly (Illus. 4.4).

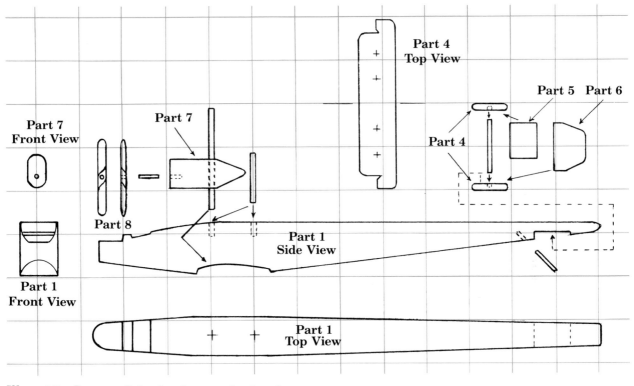

Illus. 4.2 Layout of the fuselage and related parts.
Handley Page 0/400.

ASSEMBLY

4. Mark all of the drilling points on Parts 1, 2, 3, 4, and 7 following the indicated marks in Illus. 4.2 and 4.3.
   NOTE: These holes are not to be drilled completely through the parts.

5. Use a $\frac{5}{32}''$ drill bit and drill each of the holes as indicated except the four holes on the underside of the lower wing (Part 2) near its front edge. These are to be $\frac{1}{4}''$ diameter to provide mounting holes for the landing gear (Illus. 4.3).

6. Position the lower wing (Part 2) in the notch provided at the bottom of the fuselage (Part 1). Make sure the fuselage sits right in the middle of the wing. Secure in place with carpenter's glue and $\frac{3}{4}''$ brads.

7. Cut two $1\frac{1}{4}''$ long sections from $\frac{1}{8}''$ dowel for the middle wing-to-fuselage support struts (Illus. 4.2).

8. Cut twelve $2\frac{1}{4}''$ long sections from $\frac{1}{8}''$ dowel for the wing-to-wing support struts (Illus. 4.3, end view of wing assembly).

9. Insert each of the fuselage-to-wing support struts with a drop of glue into the two holes provided in the top of the fuselage (Part 1).

10. Slide each engine (Part 7) over its own wing-to-wing support strut and glue in place so that $\frac{1}{2}''$ of the bottom of the strut protrudes (Illus. 4.2).

11. Glue these two engine–strut assemblies into the inboard forward holes in the lower wing. Align these struts so they are perpendicular to the wing (Illus. 4.2).

12. Glue the remaining ten wing-to-wing struts into the remaining holes. Align them perpendicular to the wing.

13. Glue the upper wing (Part 3) in place by inserting all of the wing support struts into the holes on the underside of the upper wing. Align the upper wing to be parallel with the lower one.

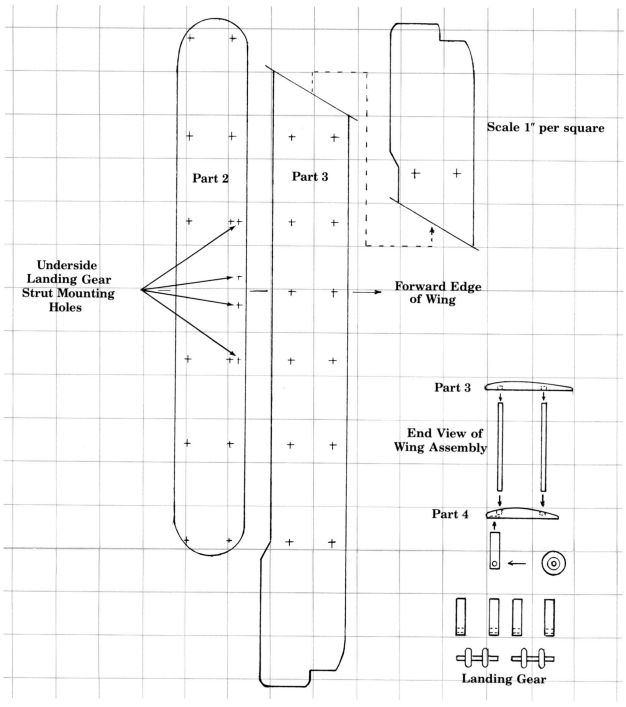

Illus. 4.3 Layout of wings. Handley Page 0/400.

14. Position one of the horizontal stabilizers (Part 4) into the notch provided at the rear bottom of the fuselage (Part 1). **NOTE:** The predrilled holes must be facing up when the aircraft is upright.

15. Cut four sections of $\frac{1}{16}''$ dowel to a $1\frac{1}{4}''$ length for horizontal stabilizer support struts (Illus. 4.2).

16. Place the middle vertical stabilizer (Part 5) and the two outboard vertical stabi-

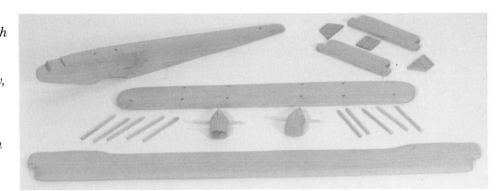

Illus. 4.4 After cutting each part to shape with a band saw, carefully sand the pieces to ready them for assembly.

lizers (Parts 6) along the lower horizontal stabilizer and fuselage. Glue the four horizontal stabilizer support struts in place.

17. Position the upper horizontal stabilizer and secure with glue by inserting the support struts into the holes provided and properly aligning the vertical stabilizers.

18. Cut four sections of ¼″ dowel to a length of 1″. These are the landing gear struts (Illus. 4.3).

19. Drill a ⁵⁄₃₂″ hole through each of these dowel sections at ¼″ from one end as shown in Illus. 4.3.

20. Cut two sections of ⅛″ dowel to a 1½″ length for the landing gear axles as shown in Illus. 4.3.

21. Slide two ¾″ hardwood toy wheels onto each of the axles.

22. Glue a landing gear strut onto each end of each of the axles, inserting the axles into the holes drilled in Step 19 at one end of the struts.

23. Attach the landing gear assemblies with glue by inserting them into the ¼″ holes on the underside of the lower wing.

24. The two propellers (Parts 8) are made from ¼″ dowel sections 2″ long. Make these propellers by following the procedure outlined in Step 4 of Project 2, page 10.

25. Cut two propeller drive shafts from ⅛″ dowel to a length of ½″ (Illus. 4.2).

26. Glue the propeller drive shafts into the holes in the forward end of each of the engines (Parts 7) as shown in Illus. 4.2.

27. Glue the propellers (Parts 8) onto the ends of the propeller shafts (Illus. 4.2).

28. This completes the *Handley Page 0/400* except for finishing (Illus. 4.5).

29. You may finish the piece with clear varnish to show the quality of your workmanship, or you can paint the aircraft in authentic colors to make a more realistic model.

30. You can display your model as it is or mount it on a desk plaque.

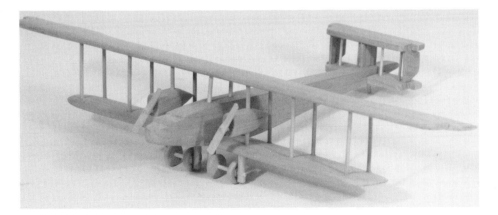

Illus. 4.5 Fully assembled Handley Page 0/400.

Curtiss R-6

Illus. 5.1

The *Curtiss R-6* was fitted with twin pontoons for water landings—mostly at sea (Illus. 5.1). First built in 1915 as an observation aeroplane, it was later fitted with machine guns and equipped to carry bombs and torpedos.

Materials List

Hardwood Stock, *¾″ × 4″ × 18″* . . . . . . *1 each*
Hardwood Dowel, *¼″ diameter* . . . . *3″*
Hardwood Dowel, *⅛″ diameter* . . . . *45″*
Carpenter's Glue . . . . *small container*

Cutting List

Part 1 . . . *Fuselage* . . . . *Make 1*
Part 2 . . . *Lower Wing* . . . . *Make 1*
Part 3 . . . *Upper Wing* . . . . *Make 1*
Part 4 . . . *Horizontal Stabilizer Halves* *Make 2*
Part 5 . . . *Vertical Stabilizer* . . . . *Make 1*
Part 6 . . . *Pontoon* . . . . *Make 2*
Part 7 . . . *Propeller* . . . . *Make 1*

Instructions

LAYOUT

1. Lay out Parts 1, 2, 3, 4, 5, and 6 on the ¾″ hardwood stock (Illus. 5.2 and 5.3). Some of these parts do not require the full ¾″ thickness and will need to be ripped to the proper thickness.

2. Cut the above parts to shape with a band saw.

3. Use your bench-mounted belt sander to form and shape the various pieces as required (Illus. 5.4).

ASSEMBLY

4. Mark all the drilling points on the above parts (Illus. 5.2 and 5.3).

5. Use a ⁵⁄₃₂″ drill bit to drill all of these holes.

    NOTE: These holes are not drilled completely through the parts. The four inboard holes in the lower wing (Part 2), however, are to be drilled completely through. These are the holes for the wing-and-pontoon support struts. Also note that the partially drilled holes are to be on the underside for the upper wing (Part 3) but along the top surface for the lower wing (Part 2).

6. Position the lower wing (Part 2) in the notch provided at the bottom of the fu-

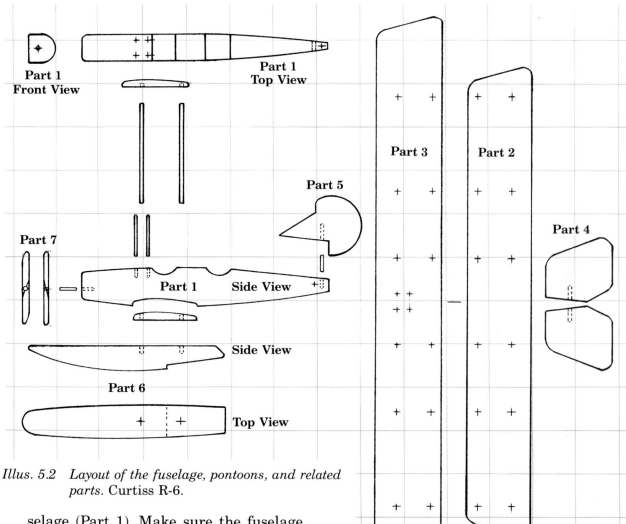

Illus. 5.2   Layout of the fuselage, pontoons, and related parts. Curtiss R-6.

Scale 1″ per square

Illus. 5.3   Layout of wings and horizontal stabilizer.

selage (Part 1). Make sure the fuselage sits right in the middle of the wing. Secure in place with carpenter's glue and ¾″ brads.

7. Cut four sections of ⅛″ dowel to a length of 1⅛″. These are for the upper wing-to-fuselage support struts.

8. Glue these four struts into the four holes provided at the top of the fuselage (Part 1). Carefully position them so that they extend to a uniform length of ⅞″ above the fuselage (Illus. 5.2).

9. Cut the eight wing-to-wing support struts to a length of 1⁹⁄₁₆″ from ⅛″ dowel.

10. Glue these struts into the eight outer most holes in the lower wing. Position each so that it is perpendicular to the wing.

11. Position the upper wing (Part 3) by inserting each of the struts into the corresponding holes along the underside of the wing (Illus. 5.5). Secure with drops of glue.

12. Now cut the four wing-and-pontoon struts from ⅛″ dowel to a length of 2½″ (Illus. 5.2).

13. Insert these struts into the four holes that were drilled completely through the

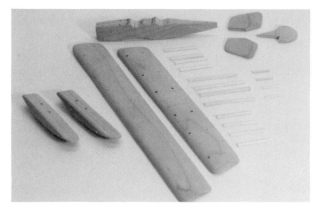

Illus. 5.4   After cutting parts to shape with a band saw, form each piece on a bench-mounted belt sander.

lower wing (Part 2), and align them with the corresponding holes in the upper wing (Part 3). Secure in place with carpenter's glue (Illus. 5.5).

14. Position the pontoons (Parts 6) and secure with glue by aligning the holes in the top side of the pontoons with the extending ends of the wing-and-pontoon struts. Make sure the pontoons are parallel with the visual midline of the fuselage and properly aligned with each other.

15. Cut a short section of ⅛″ dowel, approximately ¾″, for mounting the horizontal stabilizer halves (Parts 4).

16. Mount both halves of the horizontal stabilizer (Parts 4) by sliding the short dowel section through the hole provided at the rear of the fuselage and inserting it into the holes on the inside edge of each of the stabilizer halves (Illus. 5.2 and 5.3). Press the stabilizer halves together until they butt firmly against the fuselage.
NOTE: Check the proper fit of these parts prior to applying glue. After you are assured of a proper fit, glue these parts in place.

Align the horizontal stabilizer so that it is straight as though both halves were one piece and so that it is parallel with the wing and level with the fuselage midline when viewing the aircraft from the side.

17. Use another short section of ⅛″ dowel, approximately ⅜″ long, to mount the vertical stabilizer (Illus. 5.2). Do this in a similar way to Step 16 above, carefully checking alignment before the glue sets.

18. Make a propeller shaft from ⅛″ dowel about ½″ long.

19. Glue the propeller shaft into the hole at the nose of the aircraft and allow it to extend ⅜″ from the fuselage (Illus. 5.2).

20. Step 4 of Project 2, page 10, gives directions for shaping the propeller. Follow these directions and make the propeller (Part 7) for this project. This propeller is made from ¼″ dowel and is to be a finished length of 2″.

21. Once the propeller (Part 7) is completed, glue it in place on the propeller shaft.

22. The *Curtiss R-6* is now complete except for finishing.

23. It may be painted with authentic colors or finished to show the natural wood to suit your tastes.

24. To display your *Curtiss R-6*, you may do best to mount it on a desk plaque because its weight distribution—due to the solid-wood construction—will not allow it to sit properly on its own supports. Another idea you can always try is to carefully attach filament wires and suspend the piece in a flying pose.

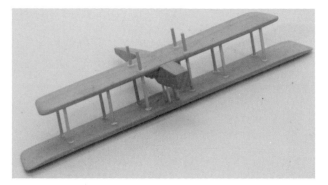

Illus. 5.5   Attach the upper wing to the wing-to-wing struts before inserting the four wing-and-pontoon struts through the lower wing. Assembly shown upside down for easy attachment and alignment.

Naval Aircraft Factory F-5L

Illus. 6.1

The *Naval Aircraft Factory F-5L* was designed as a sea-based bomber (Illus. 6.1). It was armed with eight guns and could carry four 230 lb. bombs. This multiengine biplane was remarkably stable both in the air and on the water.

Materials List

Hardwood Stock, ¾″ × 4″ × 20″ ...... *1 each*
Hardwood Dowel, ⅛″ diameter .... *30″*
Carpenter's Glue .... *small container*

Cutting List

Part 1 ... *Fuselage* .... *Make 1*
Part 2 ... *Hull* .... *Make 1*
Part 3 ... *Lower Wing* .... *Make 1*
Part 4 ... *Upper Wing* .... *Make 1*
Part 5 ... *Horizontal Stabilizer Half Make 2*
Part 6 ... *Vertical Stabilizer* .... *Make 1*
Part 7 ... *Engine* .... *Make 2*
Part 8 ... *Pontoon* .... *Make 2*

Instructions

LAYOUT

1. Lay out Parts 1 through 8 on the ¾″ hardwood stock material (Illus. 6.2 and 6.3). Parts 3 through 8 do not require the full ¾″ thickness and must be ripped to the proper thickness. Parts 5 and 6 are each ³⁄₁₆″ thick, and Part 8 is ⁵⁄₁₆″ thick. The thickness of the wings (Parts 3 and 4) and the engines (Parts 7) are shown in Illus. 6.2 and 6.3.
2. Cut all of the above parts to shape with a band saw.
3. Use your bench-mounted belt sander to form and shape each of the parts as required (Illus. 6.4).

ASSEMBLY

4. Mark each of the drilling points on all of the above parts as shown in Illus. 6.2 and 6.3. Most of these holes, however, are not drilled completely through the parts. The hole through the vertical stabilizer (Part 6) for installing the horizontal stabilizer halves and the holes through the engines (Parts 7) for upper wing support struts are the only holes that are drilled completely through.

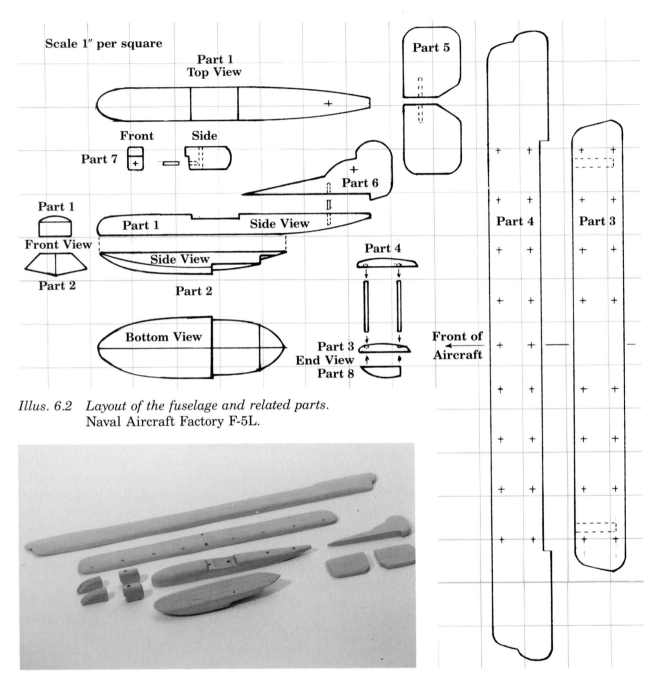

Illus. 6.2   Layout of the fuselage and related parts.
Naval Aircraft Factory F-5L.

Illus. 6.4   After cutting out the parts with a band saw and
ripping to proper thickness as necessary, form
and shape each part on a bench-mounted belt sander.

Illus. 6.3   Layout of wings.
Naval Aircraft
Factory F-5L.

5. Use a ⁵⁄₃₂″ drill bit to drill each of these holes at this time.
6. Mount the hull (Part 2) to the underside of the fuselage (Part 1) as indicated in Illus. 6.2. Secure in place with carpenter's glue.

7. Position the lower wing (Part 3) in the notch provided on the top side of the fuselage (Part 1) and glue in place (Illus. 6.2). Be careful to align the assembly so that the wing is perpendicular to the fuselage.

Illus. 6.5 Attach the engine-mounted support struts and the remaining upper wing support struts to the upper wing, making sure that each strut is perpendicular to the upside-down wing.

8. Use a short ⅛″ dowel section, approximately ½″ long, and mount the vertical stabilizer (Part 6) at the rear of the fuselage (Illus. 6.2). Position the vertical stabilizer so that it is perpendicular to the partially assembled project. Use the lower wing as a reference.

9. Use another ⅛″ dowel section to install the horizontal stabilizer halves (Parts 5) to the vertical stabilizer. Insert the short dowel section through the hole in the vertical stabilizer, and press the horizontal stabilizer halves onto both ends of the dowel until they butt firmly against the sides of the vertical stabilizer. Assemble these parts without glue to check on the fit. Once the proper fit is assured, glue these parts in place. Align the horizontal stabilizer so that it is parallel with the lower wing and level with the fuselage midline.

10. Cut eighteen upper wing support struts from ⅛″ dowel to a length of 1⅜″.

11. Slide the engines (Parts 7) onto two of the upper wing support struts. Secure with glue so that the top of the engines are ¼″ from the top end of the struts.

12. Place the upper wing (Part 4) upside down on your work bench.

13. Glue the two engine-mounted upper wing support struts into the first holes out from the middle-wing holes, towards the forward edge of the upper wing. Make sure they are set perpendicular to the wing.

14. Now glue the remaining sixteen upper wing support struts into the remaining holes, again making certain they are set perpendicular to the wing (Illus. 6.5).

15. Glue the upper wing assembly into position by inserting each of the upper wing support struts into the corresponding holes in the lower wing. Align the upper wing so that it is parallel with the lower wing.

16. Glue the two pontoons (Parts 8) to the underside of the lower wing at the locations indicated in Illus. 6.3.

17. This aircraft is propeller driven, of course, but this is a small model to make propellers for. If you do choose to make propellers, they should be 1½″ long and made following the directions of Step 4 in Project 2, page 10.

18. A model displayed in the flying mode sometimes looks more realistic without propellers, giving the illusion of spinning propellers. The propeller drive shafts, however, should be in place. These are made simply by cutting two short sections of ⅛″ dowel, approximately ⅜″ long, and inserting them into the holes previously drilled in the front end of the engines.

19. If you have chosen to make propellers, they should be installed at this time by gluing them onto the propeller shafts.

20. You are now finished with the *Naval Aircraft Factory F-5L* except for finishing. This can be done with a natural finish (Illus. 6.6) or with paint in colors that produce a more realistic portrayal of the actual aircraft.

21. This model is best displayed in a flying attitude because it has no landing gear on which to stand alone. This is easily done by making a display stand with a base of hardwood, in whatever shape you choose, with a ¼″ dowel extending about 2″.

Spad S.VII

Illus. 7.1

The *Spad S.VII* brought innovative concepts to aerial fighting machines (Illus. 7.1). It was faster than any known fighter aircraft and could hold up to continuous maneuvering without developing structural weakening that might lead to breakup.

Materials List

Hardwood Block, 1½″ × 1½″ × 8″ .... 1 each
Hardwood Stock, ¾″ × 4″ × 12″ ...... 1 each
Hardwood Dowel, ¼″ diameter .... 10″
Hardwood Dowel, ⅛″ diameter .... 30″
Hardwood Toy Wheels, ¾″ diameter ... 2 each
Carpenter's Glue .... small container

Cutting List

Part 1 ... Fuselage .... Make 1
Part 2 ... Lower Wing .... Make 1
Part 3 ... Upper Wing .... Make 1
Part 4 ... Horizontal Stabilizer Half Make 2
Part 5 ... Vertical Stabilizer .... Make 1
Part 6 ... Propeller .... Make 1

Instructions

LAYOUT

1. Lay out the fuselage (Part 1) on the 1½″ × 1½″ × 8″ hardwood block following the outlines given in Illus. 7.2.

2. Lay out parts 2, 3, 4, and 5 on the ¾″ hardwood stock (Illus. 7.2 and 7.3).

3. Use a band saw to cut each of the above parts to shape. Some of these parts do not require the full thickness of the material and must be ripped to the desired thickness. The horizontal stabilizer halves and the vertical stabilizer (Parts 4 and 5) are to be about ³⁄₁₆″ thick; the thickness for each of the other parts is indicated in Illus. 7.2 and 7.3.

4. Use a bench-mounted belt sander to form and shape these various parts as required (Illus. 7.4).

ASSEMBLY

5. Mark each of the drilling points on each of the above parts (Illus. 7.2 and 7.3).

6. Refer to the layout in (Illus. 7.2 and 7.3 and notice that some of the holes are not to be drilled completely through the parts. Also notice that the partially

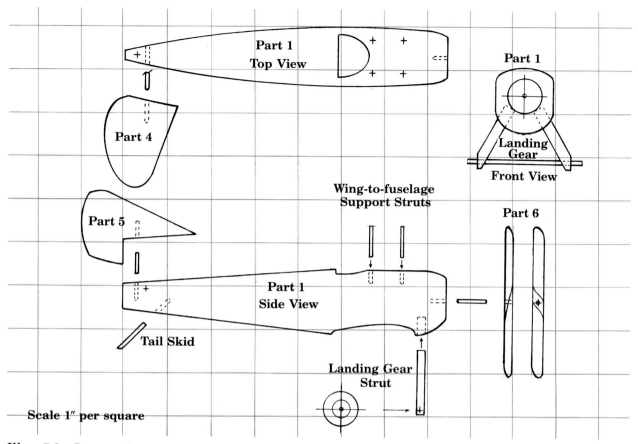

Illus. 7.2   Layout of the fuselage and related parts. Spad S.VII.

drilled holes are to be on the top surface for the lower wing (Part 2) and on the underside for the upper wing (Part 3).

7. Drill all of the holes with a $5/32''$ drill bit except for the landing gear mounting holes. These are in the lower, forward section of the fuselage (Part 1) and should be $9/32''$ (Illus. 7.2).

8. Position the lower wing (Part 2) into the notch provided in the underside of the fuselage (Part 1) and secure in place with carpenter's glue and $3/4''$ wire brads. Be sure that the wing is properly aligned with the fuselage and that the fuselage sits squarely in the middle of the wing.

9. Cut four sections of $1/8''$ dowel to a $3/4''$ length for upper wing-to-fuselage support struts (Illus. 7.2).

10. Glue these four dowel sections into the holes prepared in the top forward section of the fuselage.

11. Now cut eight wing-to-wing support struts from $1/8''$ dowel to a length of $1\,3/4''$ (Illus. 7.3).

12. Glue these support struts into the holes along the top surface of the lower wing (Part 2). Align them carefully so that each is perpendicular to the wing.

13. Glue the upper wing (Part 3) into place by inserting the upper wing support struts—already installed in the lower wing and fuselage—into the corresponding holes prepared on the underside of the upper wing. Align the upper wing so that it is parallel with the lower wing and properly positioned with respect to the fuselage.

14. Cut two sections of $1/4''$ dowel to a length of $2''$ for the landing gear struts (Illus. 7.2).

15. Use your sander and sand a bevel at one end of each of these dowel sections (Illus. 7.2). This provides you with a flat edge for

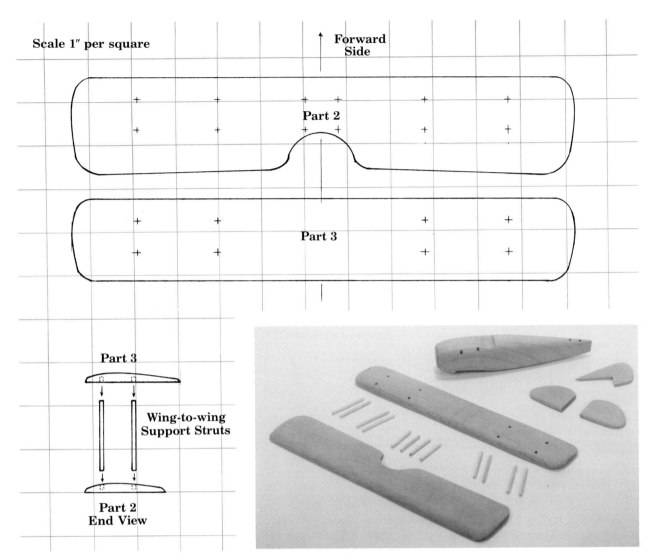

Illus. 7.3 *Layout of wings. Spad S.VII.*

Illus. 7.4 *After cutting each part to shape on a band saw, form the pieces by carefully sanding to ready them for assembly.*

drilling the landing gear axle hole and for the wheels to butt against when they are installed.

16. Drill a ⁵⁄₃₂″ hole perpendicular to the bevelled face created by the sanding operation in the previous step. Do this for both landing gear struts (Illus. 7.2).

17. Insert the landing gear struts into the larger holes prepared in the forward end of the lower fuselage. Be careful to align the axle holes. Secure in place with carpenter's glue (Illus. 7.2).

18. Cut the axle from ⅛″ dowel to a length of 2¾″ (Illus. 7.2).

19. Insert the axle through the holes prepared in the landing gear struts and allow it to extend an equal distance of about ⅜″ from either strut (Illus. 7.2). Secure with carpenter's glue.

20. Install the horizontal stabilizer halves (Parts 4) by using a short ⅛″ dowel section, about 1″ long. Pass this dowel section through the hole in the aft section of the fuselage and press the horizontal stabi-

lizer halves onto each end until they butt firmly against the fuselage. After you are assured of a proper fit, glue these parts in place. Align the horizontal stabilizer so that it is straight as one piece and so that it is parallel with the wings and level with the midline of the fuselage.

21. Mount the vertical stabilizer by using a ¾″ length of ⅛″ dowel section as an alignment pin as shown in Illus. 7.2. Glue into position.

22. Make a tail skid from ⅛″ dowel as shown in Illus. 7.2. Glue the skid into the hole prepared at the aft underside of the fuselage.

23. Use a ⅝″ center bore drill to counter set the engine area at the nose of the aircraft to a depth of approximately ⅛″ (Illus. 7.2).

24. Cut a propeller drive shaft, to a length of ¾″, from ⅛″ dowel. Glue it into the hole in the nose of the aircraft so that it is allowed to extend past the nose by approximately ½″ (Illus. 7.2).

25. Make a propeller following the instructions in Step 4 of Project 2, page 10. The propeller for this project should be 3¼″ long (Illus. 7.2).

26. Mount the propeller onto the drive shaft with a drop of carpenter's glue.

27. Install the ¾″ diameter hardwood toy wheels onto the axle ends with carpenter's glue.

28. Your model of the *Spad S.VII* is now completed except for finishing (Illus. 7.5). You may choose to finish it with a natural wood finish or with paint in authentic colors to add a touch of realism.

29. Your *Spad S.VII* can be displayed as a freestanding model or mounted on a desk or wall plaque.

Illus. 7.5 Fully assembled Spad S.VII.

· 4 ·
LATER YEARS OF WORLD WAR I

DH-4
Liberty Plane

Illus. 8.1

The *DH-4 Liberty Plane*, first built in 1917, became a workhorse of the later World War I years (Illus. 8.1). Its use continued through the mid 20s. It had a powerful 400 hp, V-12 water-cooled engine that made it faster and stronger than many of the aircraft of its era.

Materials List

Hardwood Stock, ¾" × 4" × 15" ...... *1 each*
Hardwood Dowel, ¼" diameter .... *3"*
Hardwood Dowel, ⅛" diameter .... *30"*
Hardwood Toy Wheels, ¾" diameter ... *2 each*
Carpenter's Glue .... *small container*

Cutting List

Part 1 ... *Fuselage* .... *Make 1*
Part 2 ... *Wing* .... *Make 2*
Part 3 ... *Horizontal Stabilizer* ...... *Make 1*
Part 4 ... *Vertical Stabilizer* .... *Make 1*
Part 5 ... *Landing Gear Strut* .... *Make 2*
Part 6 ... *Propeller* .... *Make 1*

Instructions

LAYOUT

1. Lay out Parts 1 through 5 on the ¾" hardwood stock (Illus. 8.2 and 8.3).

2. Some of these parts do not require the full thickness of the material and must be ripped to the proper thickness. The stabilizers and the landing gear struts (Parts 3, 4, & 5) are about ³⁄₁₆" in thickness; the thickness of the other parts is indicated in Illus. 8.2 and 8.3. The two wings (Parts 2) are exactly the same size and shape. Use a band saw to cut one piece at full

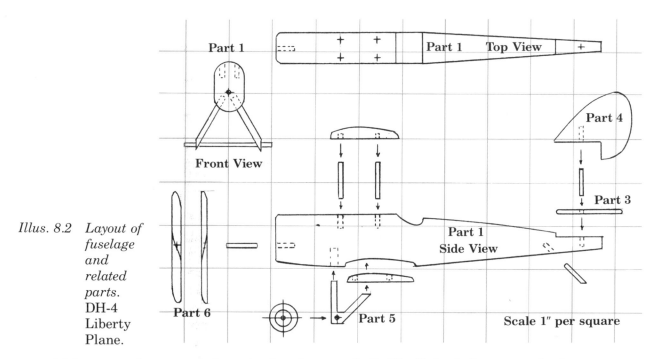

Illus. 8.2 Layout of fuselage and related parts. DH-4 Liberty Plane.

Part 1

Part 1   Top View

Part 4

Front View

Part 3

Part 1
Side View

Part 6

Part 5

Scale 1″ per square

thickness to shape, and then rip the piece into the two thinner parts.

3. Use your band saw to cut each of the other parts to shape.

4. A bench-mounted belt sander can be used to form and shape the parts as required (Illus. 8.4).

ASSEMBLY

5. Mark each of the drilling points on all of the parts as indicated by the cross marks in Illus. 8.2 and 8.3.

NOTE: Except for the holes in the horizontal stabilizer and the landing gear struts (Parts 3 and 5), these holes are not to be drilled completely through the parts.

The wings (Parts 2) are identical: designate one as the upper wing and one as the lower wing. The partially drilled holes are to be on the underside of the upper wing and on the top surface of the lower wing. Also the four holes at the middle of the wing should be omitted for the lower wing. All of the holes should be $5/32''$ diameter except for the landing gear strut mounting holes which should have a $9/32''$ diameter.

6. Drill all the holes as marked.

7. Position the lower wing (Part 2, upper surface holes, none at mid wing) into the notch provided at the bottom of the fuselage (Part 1); secure with carpenter's glue and $3/4''$ wire brads. Align the parts so that the wing is perpendicular to the fuselage and the fuselage sits squarely in the middle of the wing.

8. Cut four $1/8''$ dowel sections to a length of $3/4''$ for wing-to-fuselage support struts (Illus. 8.2).

9. Glue these struts into the holes prepared in the top forward portion of the fuselage. Allow them to extend uniformly $1/2''$ above the fuselage (Illus. 8.2).

10. Secure the upper wing (Part 2, holes on underside and at mid wing) with carpenter's glue by inserting the four wing-to-fuselage struts into the four holes near the middle of the wing. Align the upper wing so that it is parallel with the lower wing and properly positioned with respect to the fuselage.

11. Cut eight wing-to-wing support struts from $1/8''$ dowel to a length of $1\,9/16''$.

12. Glue these struts in place by positioning them from the holes drilled in one wing

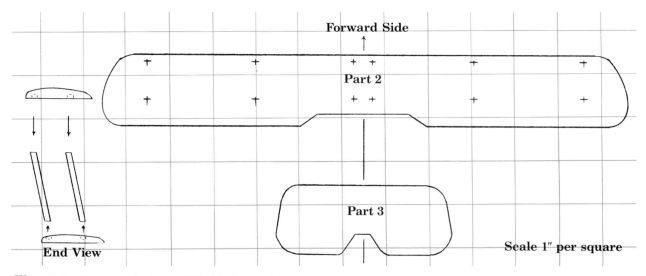

Forward Side

Part 2

Part 3

End View

Scale 1″ per square

Illus. 8.3   Layout of wings. DH-4 Liberty Plane.

to those corresponding in the other wing. The struts will tilt forward approximately 10° (Illus. 8.3, end view); they will not actually be inserted into the holes but rather use the holes simply as gluing sockets. Be very careful to maintain the parallelism of the wings.

13. The tail assembly—the horizontal and vertical stabilizers (Parts 3 & 4)—is installed in one operation as Steps 13, 14, and 15. Ensure proper fit and alignment before you apply glue. Cut a ¾″ length of ⅛″ dowel to use as a guide pin as shown in Illus. 8.2. Insert this guide pin into the hole in the bottom edge of the vertical stabilizer (Part 4).

14. Now mount the vertical stabilizer (Part 4) to the horizontal stabilizer (Part 3) by inserting the guide pin through the hole in Part 3. Press the vertical stabilizer down until it butts firmly against the horizontal stabilizer.

15. Insert the guide pin, finally, into the hole prepared in the top side of the rear fuselage. Align the horizontal stabilizer so that it is level with the wings and properly positioned with respect to the fuselage. Make sure that the vertical stabilizer is positioned perpendicular to the horizontal stabilizer and parallel to the midline of the fuselage.

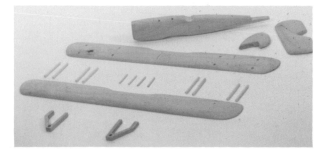

Illus. 8.4   Cut the parts to shape on a band saw and then sand each piece to the required form to prepare for assembly.

16. The landing gear struts (Parts 5) are installed by gluing them with the forward leg of the struts inserted into the ⁹⁄₃₂″ holes provided. The aft leg of the struts is simply butted against the underside of the lower wing with a drop of glue to secure them in place (Illus. 8.2). Check the proper positioning of the landing gear struts before the glue sets.

17. Cut a ⅛″ dowel section to a length of 2¼″ for the landing gear axle.

18. Install the axle by passing it through the previously drilled axle holes and allowing it to extend equally at each end, about ¼″ (Illus. 8.2, front view).

19. Cut a ⅛″ dowel section to a ⅞″ length for the tail skid. Install the tail skid with a drop of glue as shown in Illus. 8.2.

20. Cut a ¾″ length of ⅛″ dowel for the propeller drive shaft.

21. Glue the propeller drive shaft into the hole prepared at the nose of the aircraft so that it extends ½" (Illus. 8.2).
22. The propeller is 2¼" long and is made by following the directions in Step 4 of Project 2, page 10.
23. Glue the propeller onto the drive shaft.
24. Attach the two ¾" diameter hardwood toy wheels to the protruding ends of the axle with a drop of glue.

25. The construction of your *DH-4 Liberty Plane* is now complete.
26. This project can be painted with authentic colors or given a natural finish to suit your tastes.
27. Display the *DH-4 Liberty Plane* as a free-standing model or mounted on a desk or wall plaque. For a desk or wall plaque a small brass name plate adds an elegant touch.

Sopwith Camel **Project 9**

Illus. 9.1

The famous *Sopwith Camel* was first flown in 1917 but it very quickly became a viable Allied threat to enemy forces in World War I (Illus. 9.1). It was quite fast and possessed excellent maneuverability for its day. This fighter in the hands of the Canadian pilot, Captain Roy Brown, is credited with bringing an end to "The Red Baron," the great Manfred von Richthofen. The Red Baron flew the *Fokker Dr. I Triplane* (see page 41).

Materials List

Hardwood Block, 1½" × 2" × 10" .... *1 each*
Hardwood Stock, ¾" × 5" × 16" ...... *1 each*
Hardwood Dowel, ⅜" diameter .... *5"*
Hardwood Dowel, ¼" diameter .... *4"*
Hardwood Dowel, ⅛" diameter .... *20"*
Hardwood Toy Wheels, 1¼" diameter 2 each
Carpenter's Glue .... *small container*

Cutting List

Part 1 . . . Fuselage .... *Make 1*
Part 2 . . . Lower Wing .... *Make 1*
Part 3 . . . Upper Wing .... *Make 1*
Part 4 . . . Horizontal Stabilizer ...... *Make 1*
Part 5 . . . Vertical Stabilizer .... *Make 1*
Part 6 . . . Landing Gear Strut .... *Make 2*
Part 7 . . . Propeller .... *Make 1*

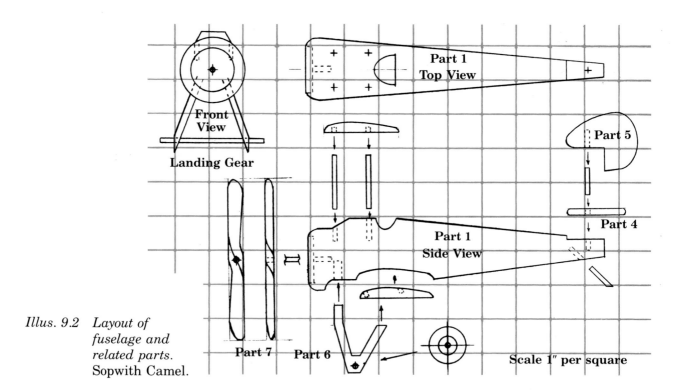

Illus. 9.2   Layout of fuselage and related parts. Sopwith Camel.

Instructions

LAYOUT

1. Lay out the fuselage (Part 1) on the hardwood block (Illus. 9.2).
2. Lay out Parts 2 through 6 on the ¾″ hardwood stock (Illus. 9.2 and 9.3). These parts do not require the full ¾″ thickness and will need to be ripped to the appropriate thickness. The vertical stabilizer (Part 5) should be ripped to a thickness of ³⁄₁₆″; all of the other parts have the thickness indicated in Illus. 9.2 and 9.3.
3. Use a band saw to cut the above parts to shape.
4. A bench-mounted belt sander can be used to shape and form the parts as required (Illus. 9.4).

ASSEMBLY

5. Mark all of the drilling points on each of the parts as indicated by the cross marks in Illus. 9.2 and 9.3.
6. **NOTE:** The holes are to be drilled only partially through the parts. The only exceptions to this are the axle holes near

the bottom of the landing gear struts (Parts 6), the guide pinhole through the middle of the horizontal stabilizer (Part 4), and the hole in the propeller (Part 7). Note also that the partially drilled holes are to be on the top surface of the lower wing (Part 2) but on the underside of the upper wing (Part 3).

7. Use a ⁵⁄₃₂″ drill bit to drill each of these holes except for the landing gear strut mounting holes in the bottom forward section of the fuselage (Part 1) and the axle holes at the bottom of the landing gear struts (Parts 6). These exceptions are to be drilled with a ⁹⁄₃₂″ drill.
8. Use a ⅞″ center bore drill to counter set the engine area to a depth of ⅛″ as shown in Illus. 9.2.
9. Position the lower wing (Part 2) into the notch provided in the underside of the fuselage (Part 1), and secure it in place with carpenter's glue and ¾″ wire brads. Be careful to align the wing so that it is perpendicular with the fuselage, and make sure the fuselage sits squarely in the middle of the wing.

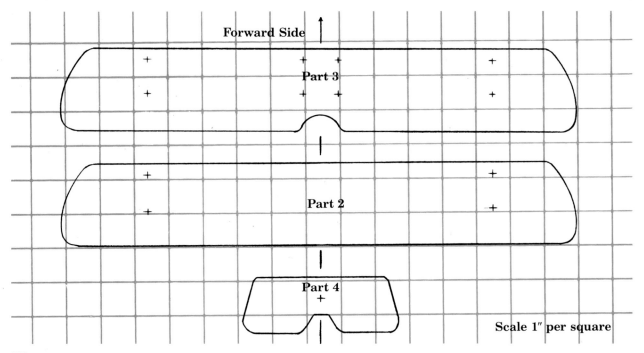

Illus. 9.3   Layout of wings. Sopwith Camel.

10. Cut four ⅛″ dowel sections to a length of 1¼″ for the wing-to-fuselage support struts (Illus. 9.2).

11. Insert these struts into the four holes prepared in the top of the fuselage (Part 1). Set them at a depth so that they extend to a uniform length of ⅞″ above the flat portion of the hump in the forward section of fuselage (Illus. 9.2).

12. Install the upper wing (Part 3) by gluing it onto the wing-to-fuselage support struts, inserting the struts into the corresponding holes in the underside of the wing (Illus. 9.2).

13. Cut four wing-to-wing support struts from ⅛″ dowel to a length of 2⅜″.

14. Glue the wing-to-wing support struts in place by positioning them from the holes drilled in the outer portion of one wing to those corresponding in the other wing. The struts will tilt forward approximately 25°; they will not actually be inserted into the holes but rather use them simply as gluing sockets. Be careful to maintain the parallelism of the wings.

15. Assemble the landing gear by gluing the

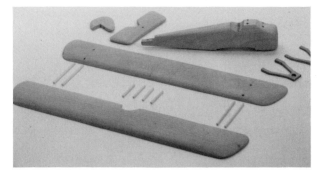

Illus. 9.4   Cut the parts to shape with a band saw, and follow by sanding each piece to the required form to prepare for assembly.

longer leg of the landing gear struts (Parts 6) into the landing gear strut mounting holes prepared in the forward lower fuselage. The shorter leg of the landing gear strut is simply glued against the underside of the lower wing (Illus. 9.2). Position the struts so that they are in proper alignment with respect to the partially assembled aircraft.

16. Insert a 3½″ long, ¼″ diameter dowel section into the landing gear axle holes so that it extends an equal amount on either end (Illus. 9.2).

17. Glue a 1¼″ diameter hardwood toy wheel to each end of the ¼″ axle.
18. Make a ¾″ length of ⅛″ dowel to serve as the tail skid. Install it into the hole on the underside of the aft fuselage (Illus. 9.2).
19. Assemble the horizontal and vertical stabilizers (Parts 4 and 5) as a unit and glue them in place using a ¾″ section of ⅛″ dowel as a guide pin as shown in Illus. 9.2. Align this assembly properly with respect to the fuselage and wings.
20. Make a propeller from ⅜″ dowel following the instructions in Step 4 of Project 2, page 10.
21. Install the propeller onto a propeller drive shaft made from a 1″ length of ⅛″ dowel. Insert the drive shaft into the hole prepared in the nose of the aircraft (Illus. 9.2).
22. Except for finishing, this completes your *Sopwith Camel*. You can paint the aircraft in authentic colors or emphasize the workmanship with a natural wood finish.
23. The finished piece can be displayed nicely mounted on a hardwood desk plaque or freestanding as it is.

Royal Aircraft Factory SE-5a

Project 10

Illus. 10.1

The *Royal Aircraft Factory SE-5a* reached the field in 1918 and quickly became a strong weapon for the Allies against enemy forces (Illus. 10.1). It scored many victories during World War I on its tour of duty as an Allied aerial fighter.

Materials List

Hardwood Block, 1¼″ × 2″ × 9″	1 each
Hardwood Stock, ¾″ × 4″ × 14″	1 each
Hardwood Dowel, ¼″ diameter	12″
Hardwood Dowel, ⅛″ diameter	25″
Hardwood Toy Wheels, ¾″ diameter	2 each
Carpenter's Glue	small container

Cutting List

Part 1	Fuselage	Make 1
Part 2	Lower Wing	Make 1
Part 3	Upper Wing	Make 1
Part 4	Horizontal Stabilizer	Make 1
Part 5	Vertical Stabilizer	Make 1
Part 6	Propeller	Make 1

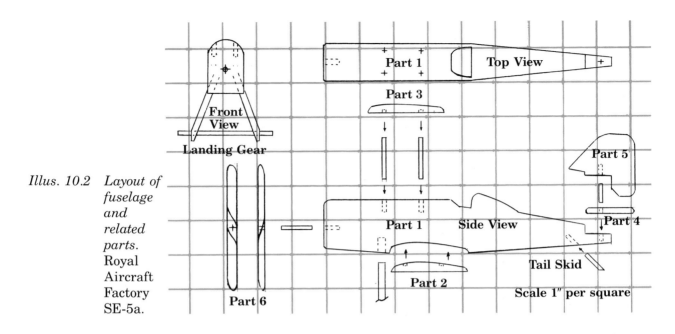

Illus. 10.2 Layout of fuselage and related parts. Royal Aircraft Factory SE-5a.

Instructions

LAYOUT

1. Lay out the fuselage (Part 1) on the hardwood block (Illus. 10.2).
2. Lay out parts 2 through 5 on the ¾" hardwood stock (Illus. 10.2 and 10.3). Keep in mind that these parts do not require the full ¾" thickness and must be ripped to the proper thickness. The thickness of all the parts is indicated in Illus. 10.2 and 10.3 except the vertical stabilizer (Part 5) that has a thickness of ³⁄₁₆".
3. Use a band saw to cut all of the above parts to shape (Illus. 10.2 and 10.3).
4. The finished form of each part is obtained by using a bench-mounted belt sander (Illus. 10.4).

ASSEMBLY

5. Mark all of the drilling points on each of the parts as shown in Illus. 10.2 and 10.3.
6. The holes in the propeller (Part 6) and the horizontal stabilizer (Part 4) are the only two holes that are to be drilled completely through the parts. The other holes are to be drilled to the approximate depths shown in Illus. 10.2.
   NOTE: The partially drilled holes in the wings are to be on the top surface of the lower wing (Part 2) and on the underside of the upper wing (Part 3).
7. All of the holes are to be ⁵⁄₃₂" in diameter except for the landing gear strut mounting holes—located just forward of the lower wing notch on the underside of the fuselage (Part 1)—that are to be ⁹⁄₃₂" (Illus. 10.2).
8. Drill all of these holes at this time.
9. Position the lower wing (Part 2) in the notch prepared in the underside of the fuselage (Part 1). Secure it in place with carpenter's glue and ¾" wire brads. Align the wing perpendicular to the fuselage, with the fuselage sitting squarely in the middle of the wing.
10. Cut four wing-to-fuselage support struts from ⅛" dowel to a length of 1¼" as shown in Illus. 10.2.
11. Glue these struts into the four holes on top of the fuselage. Each strut should extend ⅞" above the top of the fuselage.
12. Position the upper wing (Part 3) in place by inserting the four wing-to-fuselage support struts into the corresponding holes on the underside of the wing. Align the upper wing so that it is parallel with the lower wing and in proper position with respect to the fuselage.

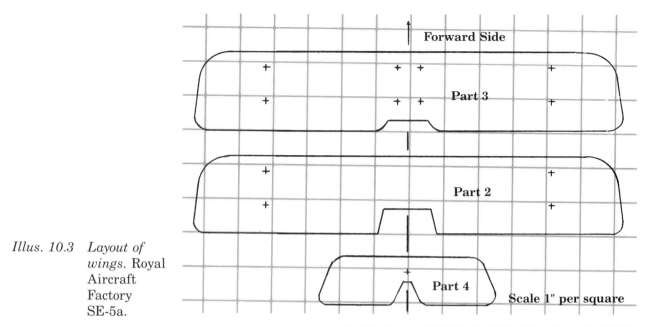

Illus. 10.3 Layout of wings. Royal Aircraft Factory SE-5a.

Forward Side

Part 3

Part 2

Part 4

Scale 1″ per square

13. Cut four wing-to-wing support struts from ⅛″ dowel to a length of 2¼″.

14. Glue these struts in place by positioning them at the holes near the end of each wing. The struts will tilt forward at approximately 30°; they will not actually be inserted into the holes but rather use them simply as gluing sockets.

15. Cut the two landing gear struts from ¼″ dowel to a length of 2″. One end of each strut is sanded at a bevel so that the bevelled edge will be perpendicular to the lower wing. Drill a ⁵⁄₃₂″ hole at ¼″ from the bevelled end and perpendicular to the flat area of the bevel (Illus. 10.2).

16. Insert the landing gear struts into the prepared holes and align the bevelled sides so that they face outward (Illus. 10.2, front view).

17. Cut a section of ⅛″ dowel to a length of 2¾″ for the axle.

18. Insert the axle into the holes in the landing gear struts so that it extends equally from both sides (Illus. 10.2, front view).

19. Attach the ¾″ hardwood toy wheels to each end of the axle.

20. Assemble the horizontal and vertical stabilizers (Parts 4 & 5) using a ¾″ length of ⅛″ dowel as a guide pin. Glue this assem-

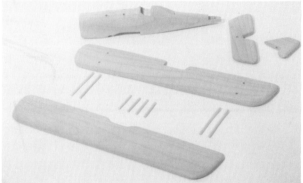

Illus. 10.4 After cutting all the parts to shape with a band saw, sand each part to the required form to prepare for assembly.

bly in place at the tail of the aircraft (Illus. 10.2). Be careful to align the tail assembly with respect to the wings and fuselage.

21. Cut a ¾″ length of ⅛″ dowel for the tail skid, and glue it in the hole prepared in the tail section of the fuselage.

22. Make the propeller drive shaft from a ¾″ length of ⅛″ dowel, and insert it into the hole at the nose of the fuselage. It should extend from the fuselage about ½″.

23. The propeller (Part 6) is made from a 3¾″ length of ¼″ dowel following the instructions in Step 4 of Project 2, page 10. It

should now be glued to the drive shaft (Illus. 10.2).

24. Your *Royal Aircraft Factory SE-5a* is now complete except for finishing. It can be finished with a natural wood finish or painted with realistic colors to give a more authentic recreation.

25. This piece can be displayed mounted on a desk plaque or it can be placed as a free-standing model.

Fokker Dr. I Triplane

Illus. 11.1

The legendary "Red Baron," Manfred von Richthofen, flew this little fighter plane into the annals of history (Illus. 11.1). The *Fokker Dr. I Triplane* was one of the most maneuverable combat aircraft ever known and has become one of the most famous.

Materials List

Hardwood Block, 1½" × 1½" × 8" .... *1 each*
Hardwood Stock, ¾" × 4" × 20" ...... *1 each*
Hardwood Dowel, ½" diameter .... *2"*
Hardwood Dowel, ¼" diameter .... *12"*
Hardwood Dowel, ⅛" diameter .... *15"*
Hardwood Toy Wheels, 1¼" diameter 2 each
Carpenter's Glue .... *small container*

Cutting List

Part 1 ... Fuselage .... *Make 1*
Part 2 ... Lower Wing .... *Make 1*
Part 3 ... Middle Wing .... *Make 1*
Part 4 ... Upper Wing .... *Make 1*
Part 5 ... Horizontal Stabilizer ...... *Make 1*
Part 6 ... Vertical Stabilizer .... *Make 1*
Part 7 ... Airfoil Axle .... *Make 1*
Part 8 ... Propeller .... *Make 1*

Instructions

LAYOUT

1. Lay out the fuselage (Part 1) on the hardwood block (Illus. 11.2).

2. Lay out parts 2 through 6 on the ¾" hardwood stock (Illus. 11.2 and 11.3). These parts do not require the full ¾" thickness and must be ripped to the thicknesses required. These thicknesses are shown in Illus. 11.2 and 11.3 except for the vertical

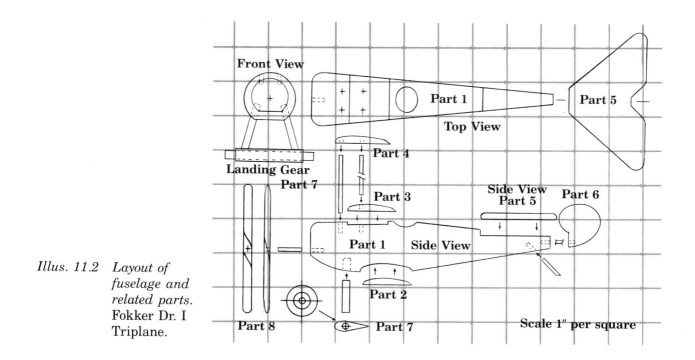

Illus. 11.2 Layout of fuselage and related parts. Fokker Dr. I Triplane.

stabilizer (Part 6) that requires a thickness of ³⁄₁₆″.

3. With the use of a band saw or jigsaw, cut all of the above parts to shape.

4. Use your bench-mounted belt sander to refine the shapes to those indicated, as shown in Illus. 11.4.

5. The airfoil axle (Part 7) is made from a ½″ dowel section by drilling a ⁹⁄₃₂″ hole through the middle lengthwise and then shaping the airfoil—or tear drop—shape on the sander (Illus. 11.2).

ASSEMBLY

6. Mark the drilling points on each of the parts as shown in Illus. 11.2 and 11.3. **NOTE:** Do not drill any of the holes until carefully reading through Steps 7 through 11.

7. All the holes are drilled with a ⁵⁄₃₂″ drill bit except for the landing gear strut mounting holes on the underside of the fuselage (Part 1), just forward of the lower wing notch. These two holes will be drilled with a ⁹⁄₃₂″ drill bit (Illus. 11.2).

8. The outboard drilling points on each of the wings (Parts 2, 3, and 4) should be marked on the underside of the wings but not drilled until directed after Step 12 (Illus. 11.3).

9. The middle drilling points on the middle wing (Part 3) should be marked on the top surface of this wing but not drilled until directed after Step 12 (Illus. 11.3).

10. Mark the middle four drilling points for the upper wing (Part 4) on the underside of this wing. These holes will be drilled only partially through the wing, approximately ³⁄₃₂″ deep (Illus. 11.3).

11. The four drilling points on the top of the fuselage should be marked but not drilled until directed after Step 12 (Illus. 11.2).

12. Now drill each of the remaining holes as indicated.

13. Position the lower wing (Part 2) in the notch prepared in the underside of the fuselage (Part 1), and secure with carpenter's glue and ¾″ wire brads. Align the wing so that it is perpendicular with the fuselage and so that the fuselage sits squarely in the middle of the wing.

14. Position the middle wing (Part 3) into the notch prepared in the top of the fuselage and secure in the same manner. Align so

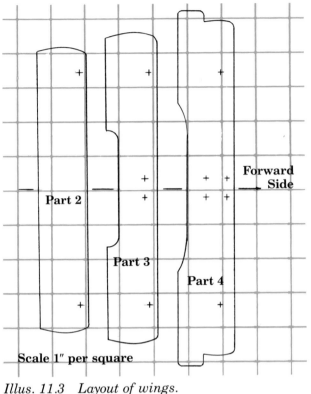

Part 2

Part 3

Part 4

Forward Side

Scale 1″ per square

Illus. 11.3   Layout of wings.
Fokker Dr. I Triplane.

Illus. 11.4   Cut the parts to shape on a band
saw or jigsaw. Refine the shapes to
the form required by using your
bench-mounted belt sander.

that it is parallel with the lower wing and properly positioned with respect to the fuselage.

15. Set the brads, and fill the holes with wood putty. Let dry and sand to a smooth finish.

16. Use a ⁵⁄₃₂″ drill bit and drill the four holes at the top for the fuselage and middle wing. These holes are for mounting the upper wing support struts (Illus. 11.2 and 11.3).

17. Cut four upper wing support struts from ¹⁄₈″ dowel to a length of 1⁵⁄₈″.

18. Glue these struts into the holes just drilled, and position them so that they extend 1⁷⁄₁₆″ above the fuselage and are perpendicular to both the fuselage and middle wing.

19. Install the upper wing (Part 4) by gluing it to the support struts; insert the struts into the corresponding holes in the underside of the wing. Make sure the upper

wing (Part 4), the other wings, and the fuselage are in proper alignment.

20. Turn the partially completed aircraft upside down on your workbench, and drill the holes previously marked on the outboard end of the wings. Do this in one continuous operation by drilling through the bottom wing, through the middle wing, and partially through the top wing. Be sure to drill each wing at the point marked. The drill will pass through each of the parts at approximately a 30° angle. These holes will be used to install the wing-to-wing support struts; this drilling method will allow the struts to pass from wing to wing at the proper forward-tilting angle.

21. Cut two wing-to-wing support struts from ¹⁄₈″ dowel to a length of 3″.

22. Install the wing-to-wing support struts by passing them completely through the holes drilled in Step 20 and securing in place with glue. Carefully check the parallel alignment of each of the wings with respect to each of the others and your workbench.

23. Install the horizontal stabilizer (Part 5) into the notch prepared at the rear of the fuselage. Secure with glue and one ½″ wire brad placed near the forward edge of the stabilizer. Align properly with the rest of the project (Illus. 11.2).

24. Install the vertical stabilizer (Part 6) with the use of a short guide pin as shown in Illus. 11.2, side view. The guide pin is a ½" length of ⅛" dowel.

25. Cut two sections of ¼" dowel to a length of 1⅜" to make the landing gear struts (Illus. 11.2).

26. Install the landing gear struts by gluing them into the holes provided. They should each extend 1" below the bottom of the fuselage.

27. The bottom ends of the landing gear struts should now be sanded so that they are parallel with the bottom of the lower wing. This can be done on the bench-mounted belt sander (Illus. 11.2, front view).

28. Glue the airfoil axle (Part 7) to the landing gear struts (Illus. 11.2, front view).

29. Pass a 3" length of ¼" dowel through the hole in the airfoil axle and secure a 1¼"-diameter hardwood toy wheel to each end of the ¼" dowel.

30. The tail skid is made from a ⅞" length of ⅛" dowel. Glue the tail skid in place at this time (Illus. 11.2).

31. Make the propeller drive shaft from a ¾" length of ⅛" dowel. Glue this shaft into the hole in the nose of the aircraft at this time. Allow it to extend beyond the nose by ½" (Illus. 11.2).

32. Make the propeller (Part 8) from a 4" length of ¼" dowel by following the directions provided in Step 4 of Project 2, page 10 (Illus. 11.2).

33. This completes your *Fokker Dr. I Triplane* except for finishing. The painting can be done with authentic colors, or you can preserve a natural wood finish to suit your tastes.

Dornier Flying Boat

Project 12

Illus. 12.1

The *Dornier Flying Boat* was not only the largest aircraft in existence when it was first built in 1915, but it was also the first to be constructed almost entirely of metal (Illus. 12.1). It lead the way with several ideas that are used in aircraft to this day.

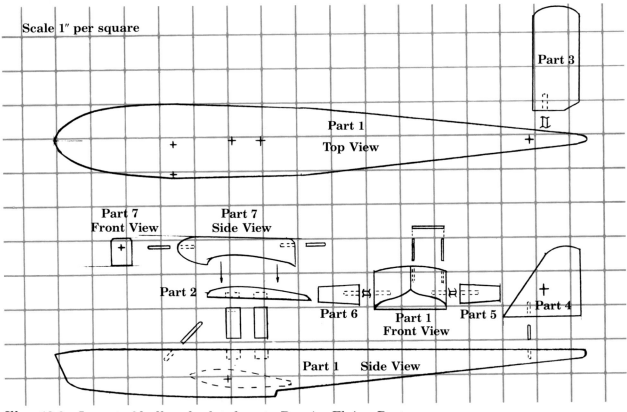

Illus. 12.2 *Layout of hull and related parts.* Dornier Flying Boat.

Materials List

Hardwood Block, 1½″ × 2¼″ × 16″ . . . 1 each
Hardwood Stock, ¾″ × 4″ × 30″ . . . . . . 1 each
Hardwood Dowel, ⅝″ diameter . . . . 3″
Hardwood Dowel, ⅛″ diameter . . . . 15″
Carpenter's Glue . . . . small container

Cutting List

Part 1 . . . Hull . . . . Make 1
Part 2 . . . Wing . . . . Make 1
Part 3 . . . Horizontal Stabilizer Half   Make 2
Part 4 . . . Vertical Stabilizer . . . . Make 1
Part 5 . . . Pontoon Stabilizer,
*   port (left) . . . . Make 1*
Part 6 . . . Pontoon Stabilizer,
*   starboard (right) . . . . Make 1*
Part 7 . . . Engine Pod . . . . Make 2

Instructions

LAYOUT

1. Lay out the hull (Part 1) on the hardwood block (Illus. 12.2).

2. Lay out parts 2 through 7 on the ¾″ hardwood stock (Illus. 12.2 and 12.3). The horizontal stabilizer halves and the vertical stabilizer (Parts 3 and 4) are to be only ¼″ thick; they will require the material to be ripped to that thickness. The wing (Part 2) is also thinner than the stock thickness; it must be ripped to a ½″ thickness.

3. Use a band saw to cut each of the above parts to their basic shapes.

4. Use a bench-mounted belt sander to finish shaping each of the parts to the final shapes required (Illus. 12.4).

ASSEMBLY

5. Mark the drilling points on all the parts as indicated in Illus. 12.2 and 12.3.

6. The holes are to be ⁵⁄₃₂″ diameter except for the two holes in the middle of the top of the hull (Part 1) and the corresponding holes in the underside of the wing (Part 2) that are to be ⅝″ diameter. These excep-

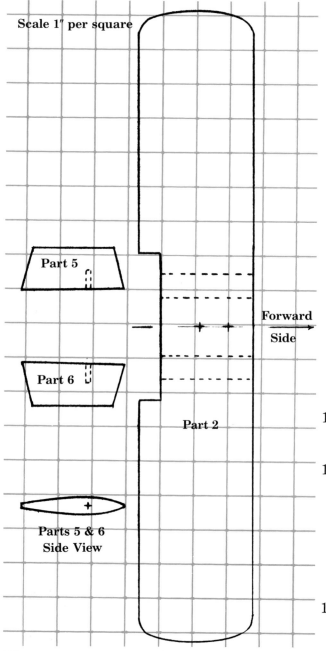

Scale 1″ per square

Part 5

Part 6

Part 2

Forward

Side

Parts 5 & 6
Side View

Illus. 12.3   Layout of wing. Dornier Flying Boat.

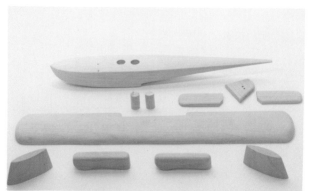

Illus. 12.4   Finish shaping each part to its final form by using a belt sander after cutting each to shape with a band saw.

8. Drill all of the holes at this time.

9. Mount each of the pontoon stabilizers (Parts 5 and 6) to either side of the hull using a 1″ section of ⅛″ dowel section as a guide pin. Press the parts onto the guide pins until they butt firmly against the sides of the hull. Use carpenter's glue to secure these parts (Illus. 12.2).

10. The windshield side posts should be cut now. They are ¾″ sections of ⅛″ dowel (Illus. 12.2).

11. Install the windshield side posts with a drop of glue for each into the holes prepared. Set them so that they extend to a uniform ½″ length above the top of the hull (Illus. 12.2). Glue a ⅞″ section of ⅛″ dowel from windshield post to windshield post. Sand these pieces flush and smooth to complete the windshield assembly.

12. Secure the vertical stabilizer (Part 4) in place by using a ¾″ section of ⅛″ dowel as a guide pin (Illus. 12.2). Position Part 4 so that it stands perpendicular to the top of the hull.

13. Mount the two horizontal stabilizer halves (Parts 3) to each side of the vertical stabilizer using a 1″ section of ⅛″ dowel as a guide pin and carpenter's glue to secure them in place (Illus. 12.2). Press these parts firmly against the sides of the vertical stabilizer; align them so that they are level as one piece and properly

tions are the mounting holes for the wing support struts (Illus. 12.2 and 12.3).

7. All of the holes marked will be drilled only partially into the parts with one exception. The hole in the vertical stabilizer (Part 4) where the horizontal stabilizer halves will be attached is to go completely through this part.

46 ◆ Making Vintage Aircraft in Wood

oriented with respect to the rest of the project.

14. The wing support struts are two 1″ sections of ⅝″ dowel (Illus. 12.2). Cut these struts to length and glue them into the ⅝″ holes drilled previously into the top of the hull. They should extend to a uniform length of ¾″ above the upper surface of the hull.

15. Glue the wing (Part 2) in place, now, by inserting the ends of the support struts into the corresponding holes in the underside of the wing. Align the wing so that it is level with respect to the rest of the project and perpendicular to the midline of the hull.

16. Cut four propeller drive shafts from ⅛″ diameter dowel to a length of ¾″.

17. Glue these drive shafts into the holes prepared at each end of the engine pods (Part 7).

NOTE: This model should be displayed without actual propellers to simulate a flying mode and also because it is too difficult to make propellers of such a small size.

18. Glue the engine pods into place at the locations indicated by the dashed lines in Illus. 12.3.

19. Your *Dornier Flying Boat* is now complete except for finishing (Illus. 12.5). You can preserve the natural wood finish or paint it with authentic colors to add realism.

20. You can display this model very nicely by showing it in a flying position. A display stand made from a ¼″ diameter dowel extending about 3″ from a hardwood base and inserted into a ¼″ hole in the bottom of the hull makes an excellent complement for exhibiting your work. A small brass name plate on the base of the stand adds an elegant touch.

Illus. 12.5 Fully assembled Dornier Flying Boat.

·5·
POST WORLD WAR I

Curtiss
P-6 Hawk

Illus. 13.1

The *Curtiss P-6 Hawk* made its airborne debut in the U.S. National Air Races at Spokane, Washington in 1927 (Illus. 13.1). Two *P-6 Hawks* were entered, and they took first and second place, recording speeds in excess of 200 mph. Purchasing agents for the U.S. military were so impressed that they placed orders on the spot, already planning to use the *Curtiss P-6 Hawk* for several diverse military purposes.

Materials List

Hardwood Block, 1¼″ × 2¼″ × 8″ .... 1 each
Hardwood Stock, ¾″ × 4″ × 14″ ...... 1 each
Hardwood Dowel, ¼″ diameter .... 10″
Hardwood Dowel, ⅛″ diameter .... 12″
Hardwood Toy Wheels, ¾″ diameter ... 2 each
Carpenter's Glue .... small container

Cutting List

Part 1 ... Fuselage .... Make 1
Part 2 ... Lower Wing, right .... Make 1
Part 3 ... Lower Wing, left .... Make 1
Part 4 ... Upper Wing .... Make 1
Part 5 ... Horizontal Stabilizer Half Make 2
Part 6 ... Vertical Stabilizer .... Make 1
Part 7 ... Wheel Spat .... Make 2
Part 8 ... Propeller .... Make 1

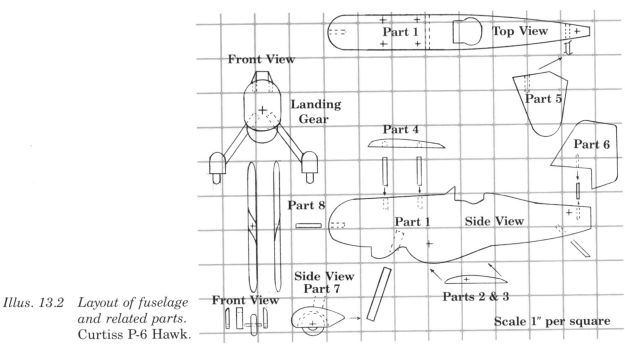

Illus. 13.2   Layout of fuselage and related parts. Curtiss P-6 Hawk.

Instructions

LAYOUT

1. Lay out the fuselage (Part 1) on the hard-wood block (Illus. 13.2).
2. Lay out Parts 2 through 7 on the ¾" hard-wood stock. These parts do not require the full ¾" thickness of the material and must be ripped to the appropriate thicknesses as shown in Illus. 13.2 and 13.3. The thickness for the horizontal and vertical stabilizers (Parts 5 and 6) is ³⁄₁₆"; this is not indicated in Illus. 13.2.
3. Use a band saw or jigsaw to cut all of the above parts to shape according to Illus. 13.2 and 13.3.
4. A bench-mounted belt sander can be used to form these parts to their finished shapes as required (Illus. 13.4).

ASSEMBLY

5. Mark all of the drilling points on the above parts as shown by the cross marks in Illus. 13.2 and 13.3.
6. The holes will be drilled with a ⁵⁄₃₂" drill bit with the exception of the landing gear mounting holes, which are to be ⁹⁄₃₂" (Illus. 13.2 and 13.3).
7. Drill the holes at this time.
8. Cut a ⅛" dowel section to a length of 2¼" for the guide pin for mounting the lower wing (Parts 2 and 3).
9. Install the lower wing halves (Parts 2 and 3), with carpenter's glue, by passing the guide pin through the hole in the side of the fuselage near the middle and pressing the lower wing halves together along the guide pin until they butt firmly against the sides of the fuselage. Align these parts—as one piece—properly with respect to the fuselage.
10. Cut four wing-to-fuselage support struts from ⅛" dowel to a length of ⅞".
11. Glue these struts into the holes prepared in the top of the fuselage, and make sure that they extend to a uniform length of ⅝" (Illus. 13.2).
12. Install the upper wing (Part 4) with carpenter's glue by fitting the four holes prepared in the underside of the wing onto the ends of the support struts. Align the upper wing so that it is parallel with the lower wing and perpendicular to the fuselage.
13. Install the horizontal stabilizer halves (Parts 5) with the use of a guide pin cut

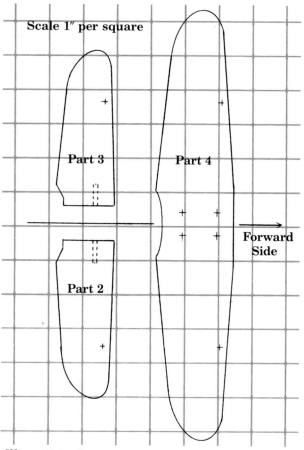

Scale 1″ per square

Part 3

Part 4

Part 2

Forward
Side

Illus. 13.3   Layout of wings. Curtiss P-6 Hawk.

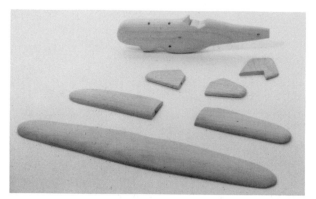

Illus. 13.4   Finish each shape to its required form by sanding after each part is cut to shape on a jigsaw or band saw.

Illus. 13.5   Wheel spat (Part 7) as constructed from several thin sections to give a wheel that can roll.

from ⅛″ dowel to a length of 1″. Follow the same guidelines used for the lower wing halves in Step 9 above (Illus. 13.2, top view).

14. The vertical stabilizer (Part 6) is also installed using a short guide pin and carpenter's glue as shown in Illus. 13.2, side view. Check the alignment so that it stands perpendicular to the horizontal stabilizer and parallel with the fuselage.

15. Cut two sections of ¼″ dowel for landing gear struts to a length of 1¾″. Sand one end to a bevel so that when the struts are installed, the flat side will be perpendicular to the lower wing (Illus. 13.2).

16. Glue the landing gear struts in place.

17. The wheel spats (Parts 7) can be made in one of two ways. They can be made in sections as shown in Illus. 13.5 or in one piece. The sectional construction will al-

low the wheel to roll. The one-piece construction simply has a section of wheel glued to the bottom to give the proper appearance. The one-piece method is a bit easier, especially when working with small parts. This method is presented in Steps 10 and 11 and also shown in Illus. 20.2 of Project 20, the *Boeing P-26 "Peashooter"* (page 69).

18. Glue the completed wheel spats and wheels to the bevelled side of the landing gear struts (Illus. 13.2). Carefully position them so that the aircraft will sit level.

19. Insert a ¾″ length of ⅛″ dowel into the landing skid mounting hole with a drop of glue (Illus. 13.2).

20. Glue another ¾″ length of ⅛″ dowel into the propeller drive shaft hole (Illus. 13.2).

21. Make a 4″ long propeller from ¼″ dowel stock following the directions provided in Step 4 of Project 2, *The Wright Flyer* (page 10).

22. Your *Curtiss P-6 Hawk* biplane is now complete and ready for finishing. It may be painted with authentic colors or given a natural wood finish.

23. Display this biplane freestanding or mount it on a desk plaque.

Ford Tri-Motor Project 14

Illus. 14.1

The *Ford Tri-Motor*, as implied by its name, was equipped with three 420-hp, nine-cylinder radial engines (Illus. 14.1). It has been used for military transport, mail carrying, and passenger service by commercial airlines. It was built in the 1920s and was in regular use for many years thereafter. Surprisingly there are some still flying today.

Materials List
Hardwood Stock, ¾″ × 4″ × 14″ . . . . . . *1 each*
Hardwood Dowel, ⅝″ diameter . . . . *3″*
Hardwood Dowel, ⅛″ diameter . . . . *12″*
Hardwood Toy Wheels, ¾″ diameter . . . *5 each*
Carpenter's Glue . . . . *small container*

Cutting List
Part 1 . . . Fuselage . . . . *Make 1*
Part 2 . . . Wing . . . . *Make 1*
Part 3 . . . Horizontal Stabilizer Half *Make 2*
Part 4 . . . Vertical Stabilizer . . . . *Make 1*
Part 5 . . . Engine Pod . . . . *Make 2*

Instructions

LAYOUT
1. Lay out Parts 1 through 4 on the ¾″ hardwood stock (Illus. 14.2 and 14.3).

NOTE: Some of these parts do not require the full ¾″ thickness and must be ripped to the proper thickness. The horizontal stabilizer halves and the vertical stabilizer (Parts 3 and 4) should be 3⁄16″ thick; each of the other parts has the thickness indicated in Illus. 14.2 and 14.3.

2. Use a band saw or jigsaw to cut each of these parts to shape.

3. Use a bench-mounted belt sander to finish the shaping process to the final form required (Illus. 14.4).

ASSEMBLY
4. Mark all of the drilling points as shown in Illus. 14.2 and 14.3. Drill the holes at this time.

NOTE: Don't drill these holes completely

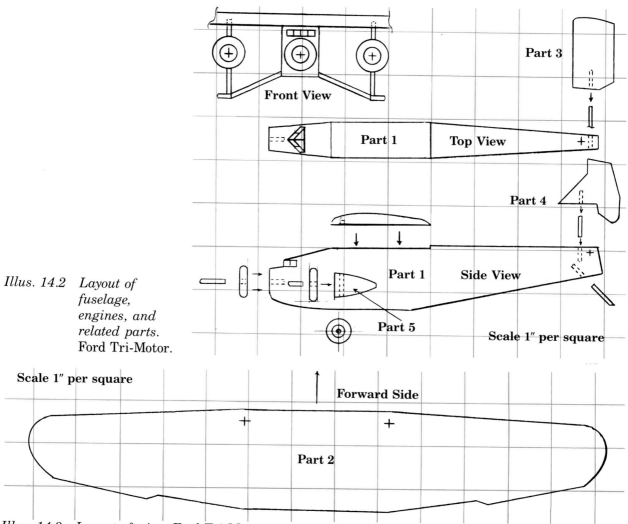

Illus. 14.2 Layout of fuselage, engines, and related parts. Ford Tri-Motor.

Part 3

Front View

Top View

Part 1

Part 4

Part 1   Side View

Part 5

Scale 1″ per square

Scale 1″ per square

Forward Side

Part 2

Illus. 14.3 Layout of wing. Ford Tri-Motor.

through the parts. Each of the holes should be ⁵⁄₃₂″ in diameter.

5. Position the wing (Part 2) in the notch prepared at the top of the fuselage (Part 1). Align it so that it is perpendicular to the fuselage and the fuselage is squarely in the middle of the wing. Secure with carpenter's glue and two ¾″ wire brads.

6. Use ¾″ long sections of ⅛″ dowel as guide pins and glue the horizontal stabilizer halves (Parts 3) and the vertical stabilizer (Part 4) in place as shown in Illus. 14.2 (top view and side view, respectively). Carefully position the tail assembly so that the parts are in proper alignment with respect to each other, the

fuselage, and the previously installed wing.

7. Make two engine pods (Parts 5) by first tapering the end of a ⅝″ dowel to form the cone shape shown in Illus. 14.2, side view. Then drill a ⁵⁄₃₂″ hole through the part, as shown by the dashed lines, for mounting to the main landing gear strut.

8. Now cut the cone-shaped section from the end of the dowel so that it is 1⅛″ long, creating the engine pod. Repeat the process for the second engine pod.

9. Cut two sections of ⅛″ dowel to a length of 2″ for the main landing gear struts.

10. Pass the main landing gear struts just cut through the hole in each engine pod

Illus. 14.4   Cut parts to shape on a band saw or jigsaw. Finish the shaping process by sanding on a bench-mounted belt sander.

until each strut extends ⅜″ beyond its engine pod. Glue in place.

11. Now insert the short end of the main landing gear strut into the hole prepared on the underside of the wing and glue in place. Align the landing gear struts so that they hang perpendicular to the wing and the engine pods are parallel to the fuselage (Illus. 14.2, front view).

12. Cut two sections of ⅛″ dowel 1½″ long for the landing gear-to-fuselage braces. Glue these braces in place as shown in Illus. 14.2, front view.

13. Make the landing gear axles by cutting two pieces of ⅛″ dowel to a length of ⅜″. Glue them to the bottom of the landing gear assembly so that they are level with the underside of the wing and perpendicular to the sides of the fuselage (Illus. 14.2, front view).

14. Cut a ¾″ length of ⅛″ dowel for the tail skid, and glue it into the hole on the underside of the fuselage towards the rear.

15. Glue two ¾″ hardwood toy wheels onto the axles.

16. The engines are also ¾″ hardwood toy wheels. Glue one to the front of each of the engine pods and one to the nose of the fuselage (Illus. 14.2).

17. Make three propeller drive shafts by cutting three sections of ⅛″ dowel to a length of ⅜″. Round one end of each with sandpaper and glue the other end into the holes in each of the wheels used as engines (Illus. 14.2).

18. This model is designed to be displayed without propellers to simulate a flying mode and also because of the difficulty in making such small propellers. Display your *Ford Tri-Motor* on a stand, and it will have the illusion of spinning propellers.

19. Except for finishing, your *Ford Tri-Motor* is now complete (Illus. 14.5). Paint your aircraft silver to represent its metal skin, or you may preserve the plane's natural wood finish so as not to conceal your workmanship.

Illus. 14.5   Fully assembled Ford Tri-Motor.

Boeing P-12

Illus. 15.1

The *Boeing P-12*, built in 1928, was an extremely agile aircraft that saw much service in the U.S. Army and Navy during the early 1930s (Illus. 15.1). It was both lighter than many of its contemporaries and able to work at higher altitudes. As well, it was quite fast.

Materials List

Hardwood Stock, ¾″ × 4″ × 10″ ...... *1 each*
Hardwood Dowel, ¼″ diameter .... *4″*
Hardwood Dowel, ⅛″ diameter .... *16″*
Hardwood Toy Wheel, 1″ diameter .... *1 each*
Hardwood Toy Wheel, ¾″ diameter .... *2 each*
Carpenter's Glue .... *small container*

Cutting List

Part 1 ... Fuselage .... *Make 1*
Part 2 ... Lower Wing, right .... *Make 1*
Part 3 ... Lower Wing, left .... *Make 1*
Part 4 ... Upper Wing .... *Make 1*
Part 5 ... Horizontal Stabilizer Half *Make 2*
Part 6 ... Vertical Stabilizer .... *Make 1*
Part 7 ... Engine .... *Make 1*
Part 8 ... Propeller .... *Make 1*

Instructions

LAYOUT

1. Lay out Parts 1 through 6 on the ¾″ hardwood stock (Illus. 15.2 and 15.3). Some of these parts do not require the full ¾″ thickness and must be ripped to the proper thickness. The horizontal stabilizer halves and the vertical stabilizer (Parts 5 and 6) are to be ³⁄₁₆″ thick; each of the other parts has the thickness indicated in Illus. 15.2 and 15.3.

2. Use a band saw or jigsaw to cut each of the above parts to shape.

3. Use a bench-mounted belt sander to shape these parts into their finished form as required (Illus. 15.4).

ASSEMBLY

4. Mark all of the drilling points on these parts as shown in Illus. 15.2 and 15.3. Each of the holes should be ⁵⁄₃₂″ in diameter. Some of the holes should only be drilled partially into the various parts. The holes in the wings should be drilled from the top side of the lower wings (Parts 2 and 3) and in the underside of the upper wing (Part 4).

5. Use a 1½″ section of ⅛″ dowel as a guide pin, and glue the two halves of the lower wing (Parts 2 and 3) in place. Align them

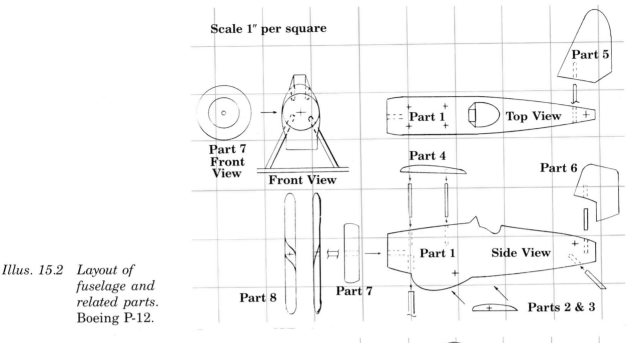

Scale 1″ per square

Part 5

Part 7
Front
View

Front View

Part 1   Top View

Part 4

Part 6

Part 1   Side View

Part 8   Part 7

Parts 2 & 3

Illus. 15.2   Layout of fuselage and related parts. Boeing P-12.

as one piece so that they are perpendicular to the fuselage.

6. Cut four lengths of ⅛″ dowel ⅝″ long for wing-to-fuselage support struts.

7. Glue these four struts into the holes in the top of the fuselage, allowing them to extend to a uniform length of ½″.

8. Mount the upper wing (Part 4) by gluing it to the four wing-to-fuselage struts. Align the struts with the corresponding holes in the underside of the wing. Align the upper wing so that it is parallel with the lower wing and perpendicular to the fuselage.

9. Use a ¾″ section of ⅛″ dowel as a guide pin to glue the two halves of the horizontal stabilizer (Parts 5) in place. Align them as one piece and level with the wings (Illus. 15.2).

10. Cut a ⅛″ dowel guide pin of ½″ length to use now to mount the vertical stabilizer (Part 6). Set the pin and the stabilizer perpendicular to the partially assembled aircraft but aligned with the fuselage midline (Illus. 15.2).

11. Cut the landing gear struts from two sections of ⅛″ dowel at a 1⅜″ length. Glue them into the holes prepared in the bot-

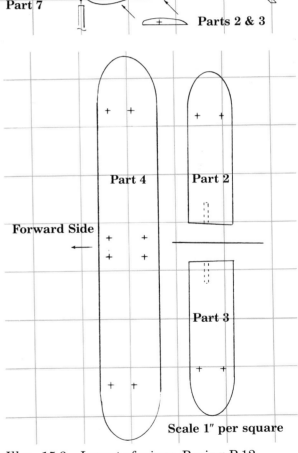

Part 4   Part 2

Forward Side

Part 3

Scale 1″ per square

Illus. 15.3   Layout of wings. Boeing P-12.

tom of the fuselage, allowing them to extend to a uniform 1″. Use the bench-mounted belt sander to sand the lower ends of these struts so that the faces are parallel with the lower wing (Illus. 15.2, front view).

12. A 2⅛″ length of ⅛″ dowel can now be glued to the landing gear struts for the axle (Illus. 15.2, front view).

13. Glue a ¾″ diameter hardwood toy wheel to each end of the axle.

14. Glue a ½″ length of ⅛″ dowel into the hole prepared in the rear of the fuselage to make the tail skid. Allow it to extend from the fuselage by ¼″ (Illus. 15.2).

15. The engine (Part 7) is simply a 1″ diameter hardwood toy wheel. Glue the engine to the nose of the aircraft (Illus. 15.2).

16. The propeller drive shaft is a 1″ length of ⅛″ dowel. Glue it into the hole at the nose of the aircraft (Illus. 15.2).

17. Make a 2½″ long propeller from ¼″ dowel stock following the instructions in Step 4 of Project 2, page 10.

18. Glue the propeller in place on the drive shaft (Illus. 15.2, side view).

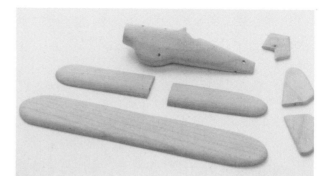

Illus. 15.4 Finish the parts by sanding each on a bench-mounted belt sander to obtain the required form after cutting out each piece to its basic shape using a band saw or jigsaw.

19. Your *Boeing P-12* is complete except for finishing. It can be painted with authentic colors to give a sense of realism or finished to preserve its natural wood finish and show the quality of your workmanship.

Curtiss F8C Helldiver

Project 16

Illus. 16.1

The *Curtiss F8C Helldiver* was introduced in 1929 as the first United States-built dive-bomber (Illus. 16.1). The *Helldiver* was an effi- cient carrier-based attack aircraft. The aircraft was capable of safely reaching targets more than 700 miles distant.

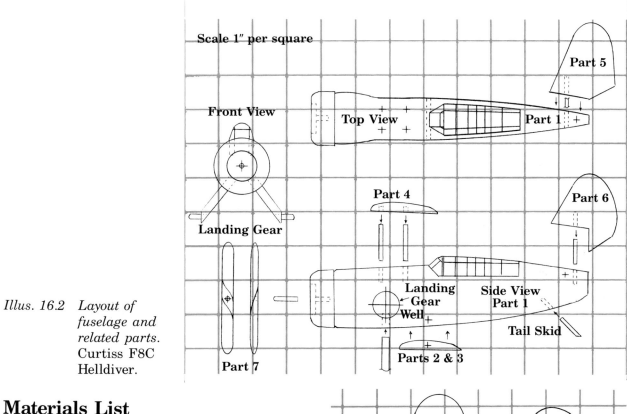

Illus. 16.2 Layout of fuselage and related parts. Curtiss F8C Helldiver.

Materials List

Hardwood Block, 1½″ × 2″ × 9″ .....*1 each*
Hardwood Stock, ¾″ × 4″ × 12″ ......*1 each*
Hardwood Dowel, ¼″ diameter ....*4″*
Hardwood Dowel, ⅛″ diameter ....*12″*
Hardwood Toy Wheels, ¾″ diameter ...*2 each*
Carpenter's Glue ....*small container*

Cutting List

Part 1 ...*Fuselage* ....*Make 1*
Part 2 ...*Lower Wing, right* ....*Make 1*
Part 3 ...*Lower Wing, left* ....*Make 1*
Part 4 ...*Upper Wing* ....*Make 1*
Part 5 ...*Horizontal Stabilizer Half* *Make 2*
Part 6 ...*Vertical Stabilizer* ....*Make 1*
Part 7 ...*Propeller* ....*Make 1*

Instructions

LAYOUT

1. Lay out the fuselage (Part 1) on the hardwood block (Illus. 16.2).
2. Lay out Parts 2 through 6 on the ¾″ hardwood stock (Illus. 16.2 and 16.3).
   NOTE: These parts do not require the full ¾″ thickness and must be ripped to

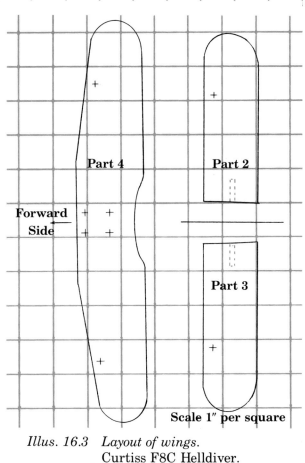

Illus. 16.3 Layout of wings. Curtiss F8C Helldiver.

the proper thickness as shown in Illus. 16.2 and 16.3. The horizontal stabilizer and the vertical stabilizer (Parts 5 and 6) are designed to be ³⁄₁₆″ thick; the thickness of the other parts is shown in Illus. 16.2 and 16.3.

3. Use a band saw or jigsaw to cut all of the above parts to shape.

4. Use a bench-mounted belt sander to form and shape these parts to their finished shape as required (Illus. 16.4).

ASSEMBLY

5. Mark all of the drilling points on the above parts (Illus. 16.2 and 16.3). All of the small holes indicated should be ⁵⁄₃₂″ in diameter; the counter set hole in the nose of the fuselage (Part 1) and the two counter set holes on the sides of the fuselage (the landing gear wells) are to be ⅞″. All of these larger holes are to be counter set by ³⁄₁₆″. Carefully read Steps 13 through 19 before drilling the landing gear mounting holes.

6. At this time drill all of the holes—except the landing gear mounting holes; they will be drilled in Step 15, if you decide to install the landing gear in the extended position.

7. Cut a piece of ⅛″ dowel to a length of 2¼″ as a guide pin. Glue the lower wing halves (Parts 2 and 3) in place by inserting the guide pin through the lower wing mounting hole and pressing the wing halves over the guide pin until they butt firmly against the sides of the fuselage. Align the lower wing halves as one piece so that they are perpendicular to the fuselage and in proper position. Tip the wing halves upwards so that the outer end of each wing is approximately ¼″ higher than the base of the wing where it joins the fuselage.

8. Cut four ⅛″ dowel sections to 1″ lengths for wing-to-fuselage mounting struts (Illus. 16.2).

9. Glue these struts into the holes at the top of the fuselage. Allow each strut to extend

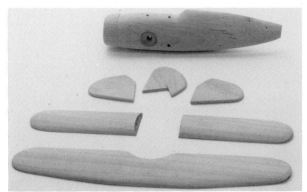

Illus. 16.4   Finish each shape to its required form by sanding after each part is cut to shape on a jigsaw or band saw.

to a uniform length of ⁹⁄₁₆″ (Illus. 16.2).

10. Install the upper wing (Part 4) by gluing it to the ends of the wing-to-fuselage struts, fitting the struts into the corresponding holes. Align this wing so that it is properly balanced over the lower wing and perpendicular to the fuselage.

11. Install the horizontal stabilizer halves (Parts 5) in the same way that the lower wing was installed, but using a guide pin cut from ⅛″ dowel to a length of about 1¼″ (Illus. 16.2). Align these parts as one piece parallel to the wing assembly and to the midline of the fuselage.

12. Using a ⅛″ dowel guide pin ¾″ long, glue the vertical stabilizer (Part 6) in place (Illus. 16.2). Align it perpendicular to the horizontal stabilizer and parallel with the midline of the fuselage.

13. The landing gear can be displayed in the extended or retracted position. If you would prefer displaying the model in the flying mode, you may want to install the landing gear as retracted. If so, do Step 14 and omit Steps 15 through 20. If you choose to have the landing gear in the extended position, omit Step 14 only.

14. To show the landing gear in the retracted position simply glue a ¾″ diameter hardwood toy wheel into each of the ⅞″ counter set holes on each side of the fuselage. Then glue a ³⁄₁₆″ section of ⅛″ dowel into the axle hole of each wheel.

15. If the landing gear is to be shown in the extended position, drill the ⁹⁄₃₂″ holes required to mount the landing gear struts as shown in Illus. 16.2, side view and front view.

16. Cut the two landing gear struts from ¼″ dowel to a length of 1½″. Bevel one end of each strut so that the bevelled face will be perpendicular to the lower wing when the strut is inserted into the mounting hole (Illus. 16.2, front view). Glue the struts in place, and align the bevelled faces properly before the glue sets.

17. Drill a ⁵⁄₃₂″ hole perpendicular to the bevelled face at the lower end of each landing gear strut for mounting of the axle (Illus. 16.2, front view).

18. Make two ⅜″ long axles from ⅛″ dowel, and glue them into the holes just drilled (Illus. 16.2).

19. Glue a ¾″ diameter hardwood toy wheel onto each axle.

20. Cut a ¾″ length of ⅛″ dowel for the tail skid. Glue it into the hole prepared at the rear underside of the fuselage (Illus. 16.2).

21. Make the propeller drive shaft from a ¾″ length of ⅛″ dowel. Glue the shaft into the hole in the nose of the aircraft, and let it extend by ⅜″ (Illus. 16.2, side view).

22. If you prefer displaying the aircraft in the flying mode, you may omit installing the propeller. The absence of the propeller gives the illusion that the propeller is actually spinning.

23. If a propeller is used, it should be 2½″ long and made following the instructions provided in Step 4 of Project 2, page 10 (Illus. 16.2).

24. Your *Curtiss F8C Helldiver* is now complete except for finishing. You may choose to paint it with authentic colors and designs, adding realism, or to preserve the natural wood finish, exhibiting your craftsmanship.

25. If you chose to make the landing gear in the retracted position then display the aircraft as though flying by placing it on a stand. If the landing gear is down, then the display can be freestanding or on a desk plaque. A small brass nameplate adds an elegant touch.

Bristol Bulldog Project 17

Illus. 17.1

The *Bristol Bulldog* was a superb fighter plane (Illus. 17.1). It had a powerful 440-hp radial engine and an unmatched ability to climb. The *Bulldog* could easily reach an altitude of 20,000 ft. in slightly more than fourteen minutes.

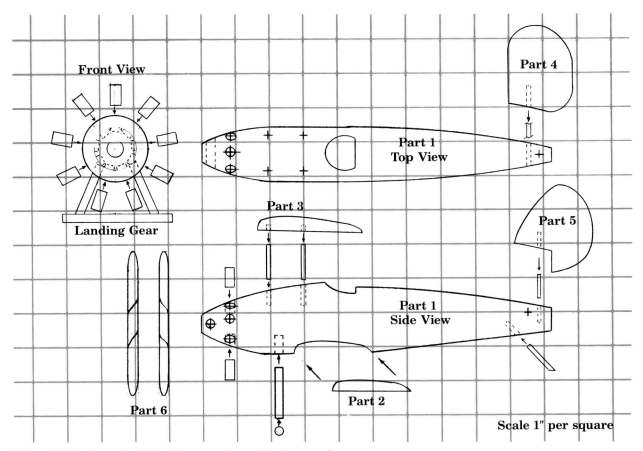

*Illus. 17.2 Layout of fuselage, engine cylinders, and
related parts.* Bristol Bulldog.

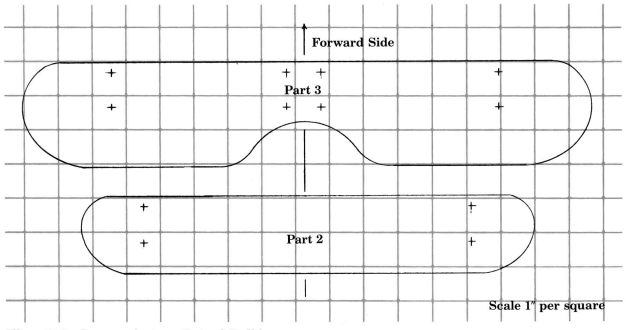

Illus. 17.3 Layout of wings. Bristol Bulldog.

Materials List

Hardwood Block 2″ × 2″ × 11″ . . . . 1 each
Hardwood Stock ¾″ × 4″ × 25″ . . . . . . 1 each
Hardwood Dowel, ¼″ diameter . . . . 25″
Hardwood Dowel, ⅛″ diameter . . . . 25″
Hardwood Toy Wheels, 1¼″ diameter 2 each
Carpenter's Glue . . . . small container

Cutting List

Part 1 . . . Fuselage . . . . Make 1
Part 2 . . . Lower Wing . . . . Make 1
Part 3 . . . Upper Wing . . . . Make 1
Part 4 . . . Horizontal Stabilizer Half Make 2
Part 5 . . . Vertical Stabilizer . . . . Make 1
Part 6 . . . Propeller . . . . Make 1

Instructions

LAYOUT

1. Lay out the fuselage (Part 1) on the hardwood block (Illus. 17.2).
2. Lay out Parts 2 through 5 on the ¾″ hardwood stock (Illus. 17.2 and 17.3).
   NOTE: These parts do not require the full ¾″ thickness and must be ripped to the proper thickness. The horizontal stabilizer halves and vertical stabilizer (Parts 4 and 5) are to be ³⁄₁₆″ thick; the thickness of each of the other parts is shown in Illus. 17.2.
3. Use a band saw to cut each of the above parts to shape.
4. Use a bench-mounted belt sander to form and shape these parts to their finished shape as required (Illus. 17.4).

ASSEMBLY

5. Mark each of the drilling points on these parts as shown in Illus. 17.2 and 17.3. The holes for the propeller, engine cylinders, and landing gear struts are ⁹⁄₃₂″-diameter holes. All of the remaining holes are to be ⁵⁄₃₂″ diameter.
6. Drill all of the holes at this time.
7. To give each wing an upward tilt—or dihedral—cut partially through along the underside halfway between the wingtips as shown in Illus. 17.4. Bend the

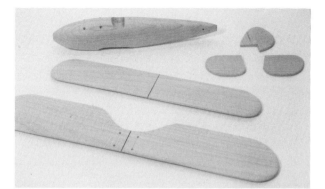

Illus. 17.4 Finish each part to its required form by sanding after each part is cut to shape on a band saw. Note partial cuts in underside of wings for dihedral.

wings upwards when gluing them in place. To prevent cracking gently boil each wing in water for about five minutes prior to bending.

8. Position the lower wing (Part 2) into the notch prepared in the underside of the fuselage (Part 1). Secure the wing in place with carpenter's glue and two ¾″ wire brads. Make sure the wing is perpendicular to the fuselage (Illus. 17.2).
9. Cut four sections of ⅛″ dowel to 1⅛″ lengths for upper wing-to-fuselage struts.
10. Glue these struts into the four holes prepared at the top of the fuselage as shown in Illus. 17.2.
11. Install the upper wing by gluing it to the wing-to-fuselage struts, inserting the struts into the corresponding holes in the underside of the wing. Align the upper wing parallel with the lower wing and perpendicular to the fuselage (Illus. 17.2).
12. Make a guide pin by cutting a 1½″ section of ⅛″ dowel.
13. Use this guide pin to glue the horizontal stabilizer halves (Parts 4) into place as shown in Illus. 17.2.
14. Use another ⅛″ dowel guide pin of ¾″ length to install the vertical stabilizer (Part 5) as shown in Illus. 17.2, side view.
15. The engine cylinders are ½″ sections of ¼″ dowel glued into the holes prepared around the nose of the aircraft. Allow

each cylinder to extend 5⁄16″ from the fuselage (Illus. 17.2, front view).

16. Cut two 1½″ sections of ¼″ dowel for the landing gear struts. Glue these struts into the holes prepared and allow each strut to extend 1⅛″ from the fuselage.

17. Sand the landing gear struts on a belt sander until they are flat on the bottom, parallel with the level aircraft (Illus. 17.2, front view).

18. Cut an axle from ¼″ dowel to a length of 3½″.

19. Glue the axle to the landing gear struts so that it extends equally at each end by about 3⁄8″ (Illus. 17.2, front view).

20. Glue a 1¼″-diameter hardwood toy wheel onto each end of the axle.

21. Glue a 1″ length of ⅛″ dowel into a slightly angled 5⁄32″ hole at the rear underside of the fuselage to add a tail skid.

22. The propeller (Part 6) is made from ¼″ dowel with a length of 4½″. It should be made following the instructions in Step 4 of Project 2 (page 10).

23. Install the propeller by gluing it into the hole prepared at the nose of the aircraft (Illus. 17.2).

24. This completes your *Bristol Bulldog* except for finishing. You may finish the aircraft to show its natural wood quality or paint it with authentic colors to make a more realistic display.

25. Display the *Bristol Bulldog* freestanding or mounted on a desk plaque.

Douglas 0-46

Illus. 18.1

In 1936 the Douglas Aircraft Company released its new model, the *Douglas 0-46* observation aircraft (Illus. 18.1). The *Douglas 0-46* had an extremely powerful 725-hp fourteen- cylinder radial engine. This high-wing monoplane routinely operated at speeds of 190 mph. It was a fast, capable airplane that became used extensively by U.S. forces.

Materials List
Hardwood Block, 1¼″ × 2″ × 10″ . . . . 1 each
Hardwood Stock, 3⁄4″ × 4″ × 25″ . . . . . . 1 each
Hardwood Dowel, ¼″ diameter . . . . 10″
Hardwood Dowel, ⅛″ diameter . . . . 25″
Hardwood Toy Wheels, 3⁄4″ diameter . . . 2 each
Carpenter's Glue . . . . small container

Cutting List
Part 1 . . . Fuselage . . . . Make 1

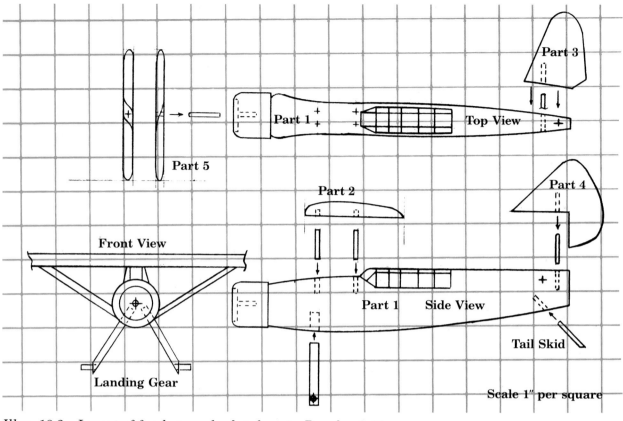

Illus. 18.2   Layout of fuselage and related parts. Douglas 0-46.

Part 2 . . . Wing . . . . *Make 1*
Part 3 . . . Horizontal Stabilizer Half Make 2
Part 4 . . . Vertical Stabilizer . . . . *Make 1*
Part 5 . . . Propeller . . . . *Make 1*

Instructions

LAYOUT

1. Lay out the fuselage (Part 1) on the hardwood block (Illus. 18.2).
2. Lay out Parts 2, 3, and 4 on the ¾″ hardwood stock (Illus. 18.2 and 18.3).
   NOTE: These parts do not require the full ¾″ thickness and must be ripped to the proper thickness. The horizontal stabilizer halves and the vertical stabilizer (Parts 3 and 4) are to be ³⁄₁₆″. The wing (Part 2) has the thickness indicated in Illus. 18.2, and it may require some special shaping.
3. Use your band saw to cut these parts to shape.
4. Use a bench-mounted belt sander to form and shape the parts as required (Illus. 18.4).

ASSEMBLY

5. Mark all of the drilling points on the various parts as indicated (Illus. 18.2 and 18.3). The holes are ⁵⁄₃₂″-diameter holes except for the landing gear strut mounting holes which are ⁹⁄₃₂″. Also the counter set engine area is done with a ⅞″ center bore drill to a depth of about ⅛″.
6. Drill each of these holes at this time.
7. Cut four sections of ⅛″ dowel to 1″ lengths for the wing-to-fuselage support struts (Illus. 18.2).
8. Glue these struts into the holes prepared in the top of the fuselage (Part 1). Make sure that they extend evenly by ¾″ (Illus. 18.2).
9. Glue the wing (Part 2) in place by inserting the wing-to-fuselage support struts

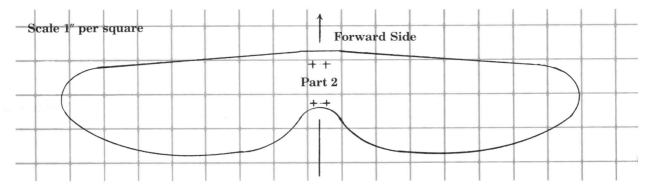

Forward Side

+ +

Part 2

+ +

Illus. 18.3   Layout of wing. Douglas 0-46.

into the corresponding holes in the under-side of the wing. Position the wing perpendicular with the fuselage and so that the fuselage is balanced beneath the wing properly.

10. Cut four 2¾″ sections of ⅛″ dowel for the wing bracing struts. Glue these in place as shown in Illus. 18.2, front view.

11. Make a 1½″ guide pin from ⅛″ dowel. Use the pin to install the two horizontal stabilizer halves (Parts 3) by inserting it through the hole prepared at the rear of the fuselage and gluing the stabilizer halves to either side. Press the stabilizer halves onto the guide pin until they butt firmly against the fuselage sides (Illus. 18.2, top view). Carefully position the stabilizer halves level with the wing.

12. Cut a ¾″ guide pin from ⅛″ dowel to install the vertical stabilizer (Part 4) in a like manner (Illus. 18.2, side view).

13. Cut two 2″ lengths of ¼″ dowel for the landing gear struts. Bevel one end as shown in the front view of Illus. 18.2 so that the bevelled face will be perpendicular to the wing when the struts are installed.

14. Carefully drill a ⁵⁄₃₂″-diameter hole ⅛″ from the end of each strut and perpendicular to the bevelled face (Illus. 18.2, front view).

15. Glue two ⅜″ lengths of ⅛″ dowel into the landing gear strut holes to form the axles (Illus. 18.2).

16. Glue the landing gear strut assemblies into the mounting holes prepared. Make

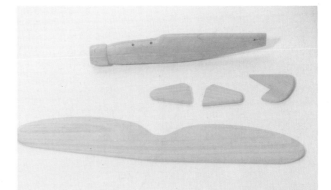

Illus. 18.4   Cut the parts to shape on the band saw. Sand each part to its required form using a bench-mounted belt sander.

sure they extend uniformly from the fuselage by 1⁹⁄₁₆″ (Illus. 18.2).

17. Glue a ¾″-diameter hardwood toy wheel to each axle.

18. Cut a 1″ long section of ⅛″ dowel for the tail skid and install it in the hole prepared in the rear fuselage (Illus. 18.2).

19. Make the propeller drive shaft by cutting a ¾″ section of ⅛″ dowel. Glue this piece into the small hole in the nose of the aircraft and allow it to extend by ⅜″ (Illus. 18.2, side view).

20. Follow the directions in Step 4 of Project 2 (page 10) to make a 4″ long propeller from a section of ¼″ dowel.

21. Glue the propeller in place onto the drive shaft (Illus. 18.2).

22. This completes your *Douglas 0-46* except for finishing. You can preserve the natural wood finish or paint the aircraft in authentic colors to add a sense of realism.

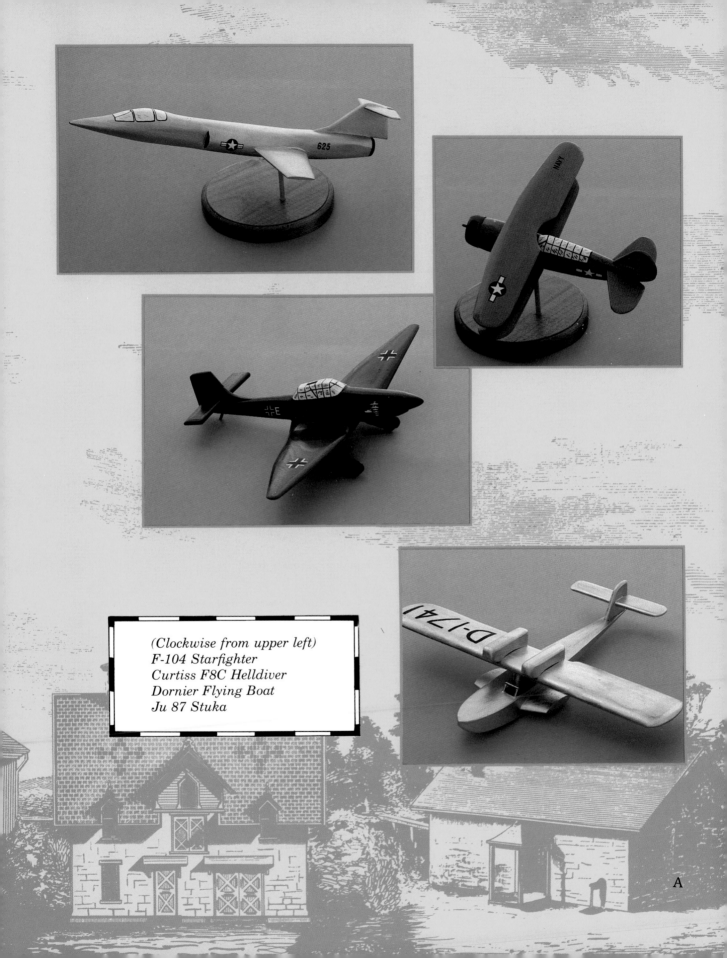

(Clockwise from upper left)
F-104 Starfighter
Curtiss F8C Helldiver
Dornier Flying Boat
Ju 87 Stuka

A

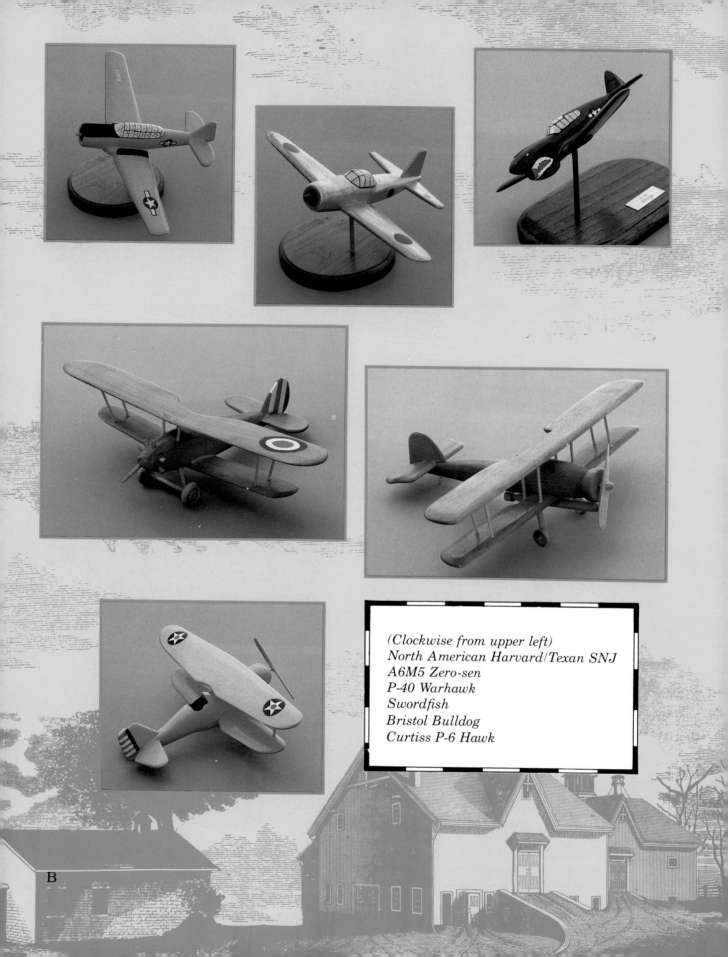

(Clockwise from upper left)
North American Harvard/Texan SNJ
A6M5 Zero-sen
P-40 Warhawk
Swordfish
Bristol Bulldog
Curtiss P-6 Hawk

B

(Clockwise from upper left)
Spad S. VII
Goodyear Zeppelin
P-38 Lightning
Fokker Dr. I Triplane
Royal Aircraft Factory SE-5a

C

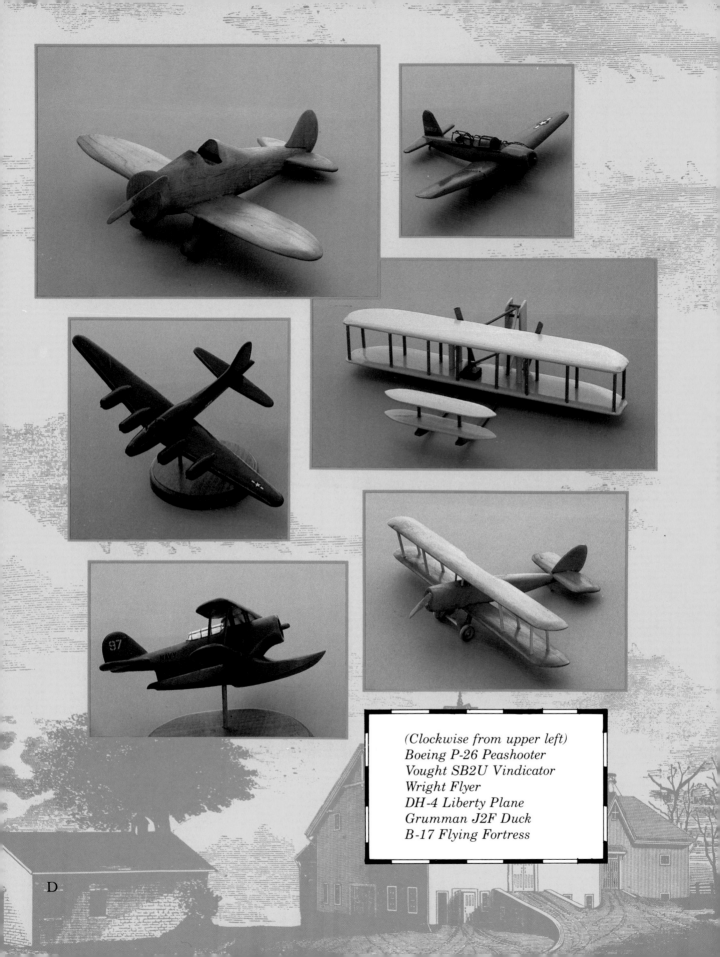

(Clockwise from upper left)
Boeing P-26 Peashooter
Vought SB2U Vindicator
Wright Flyer
DH-4 Liberty Plane
Grumman J2F Duck
B-17 Flying Fortress

D

·6·
LIGHTER THAN AIR
FOR A
MODERN CENTURY

Goodyear Zeppelin

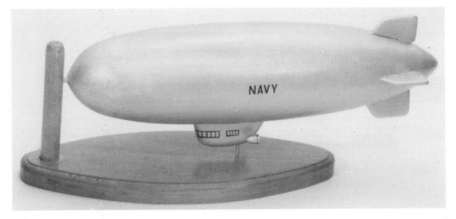

Illus. 19.1

The *Goodyear Zeppelin*, first built in 1921, enjoyed a forty year career with the U.S. Navy being retired in 1961 (Illus. 19.1). It made a wonderful observation ship particularly because the airship was capable of staying aloft for as long as forty-eight hours.

Materials List
Hardwood Block, 4½″ × 4½″ × 16″ 1 each*
Hardwood Stock, ¾″ × 4″ × 5″ . . . . . . .1 each
Hardwood Dowel, ⅜″ diameter . . . . .2″
Hardwood Dowel, ⅛″ diameter . . . . .6″
Carpenter's Glue . . . . small container

*This block can be fabricated by laminating several layers of hardwood stock.

Cutting List
Part 1 . . . Helium Envelope . . . . .Make 1
Part 2 . . . Control Fins . . . . .Make 4
Part 3 . . . Gondola . . . . .Make 1
Part 4 . . . Engine Pod . . . . .Make 2

Instructions

LAYOUT
1. The helium envelope (Part 1) is best turned on your lathe. Make a shaping template to provide better accuracy during this process. Lay out the shape of Part 1 on a piece of construction paper or thin

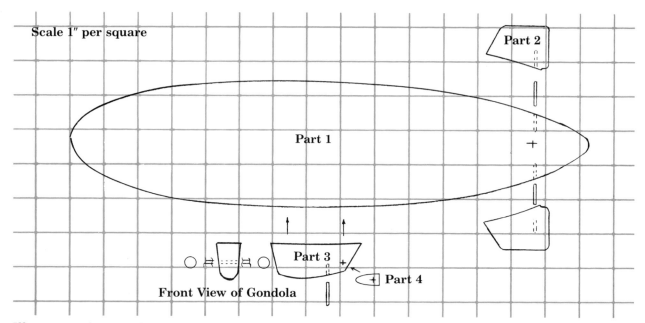

Scale 1″ per square

Part 2

Part 1

Part 3

Part 4

Front View of Gondola

Illus. 19.2   Layout of parts. Goodyear Zeppelin.

cardboard. Draw a line from end to end along the shape's midline, and cut the shape in half along this line. Now cut out one of the half shapes and use the outside piece as the turning template (Illus. 19.2).

2. Position the hardwood block in your lathe. Using the template as a guide, turn the helium envelope to its proper shape.

3. After the shape is obtained, use several grades of sandpaper to smooth the part to a fine finish while it still turns in the lathe.

4. Lay out four control fins (Parts 2) and the gondola (Part 3) on the ¾″ stock (Illus. 19.2). The control fins (Parts 2) must be ripped to ³⁄₁₆″ thickness.

5. Use a band saw to cut Parts 2 and 3 to their basic shape.

6. Now, use a bench-mounted belt sander to shape and form the finished shapes of these parts (Illus. 19.3).

ASSEMBLY

7. Draw a line radially around the aft end of the helium envelope (Part 1), 2″ from the end. Now mark the drilling points along this line so that they are 90° apart. These mark the drilling locations for the guide

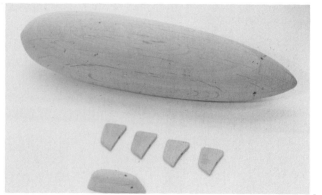

Illus. 19.3   Turn the large Helium Envelope on a lathe. Cut the control fins and the gondola on a band saw, and then sand them as required using a bench-mounted belt sander.

pinholes for mounting the control fins (Illus. 19.2).

8. Mark the drilling points on the gondola, and mark the guide pin mounting holes on the edge of the control fins (Illus. 19.2).

9. Use a ⁵⁄₃₂″ drill bit and drill each of these holes.

10. Cut four ¾″ guide pins from ⅛″ dowel. Glue the control fins in place using these pins as shown in Illus. 19.2. Align these parts so that they project from Part 1 perpendicular to each other.

11. Glue the gondola in place beneath the helium envelope (Illus. 19.2). It should be directly in line with the lower control fin and also properly aligned with the helium envelope.

12. The engine pods (Parts 4) are made from ³⁄₈″ dowel. Simply use your bench-mounted belt sander to shape the end of the dowel into the cone shape required by turning the dowel in your hands as you sand it (Illus. 19.2). Once the proper shape is obtained, mark and drill the ⁵⁄₃₂″-diameter mounting hole. Then cut off the shaped end of each dowel ½″ from the end to form each engine pod (Parts 4).

13. Pass a 1½″ length of ⅛″ dowel through the hole in the side of the gondola and allow it to extend equally from each side, approximately ³⁄₈″. Each end is an engine pod mounting strut (Illus. 19.2, front view).

14. Glue one of the finished engine pods to each end of this mounting strut (Illus. 19.2, front view).

15. The landing gear for this airship is simply a ¾″ section of ⅛″ dowel glued into the hole at the bottom of the gondola (Illus. 19.2).

16. Your *Goodyear Zeppelin* is now complete (Illus. 19.4).

17. You can preserve the natural finish or paint your airship with the more authentic aluminum color.

18. Display of this model must be done in some way to support its weight safely. A desk plaque works well, or you may choose a wall plaque with a couple of dowels securing the model from behind. This airship would also look quite well mounted on the base of a den lamp either in the landed or flying position.

Illus. 19.4 Fully assembled Goodyear Zeppelin.

·7·
LEADING UP TO
WORLD WAR II

Boeing P-26
Peashooter

Project 20

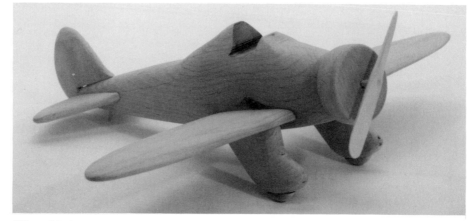

Illus. 20.1

The *Boeing P-26* was built in 1932 (Illus. 20.1). The *P-26*, which was also known as the *Peashooter*, was a very fast monoplane that was built entirely of metal. The *Boeing P-26 Peashooter* became the U.S. Army Air Corps.' primary pursuit fighter until 1939.

Materials List
Hardwood Block, 2¼″ × 3½″ × 12″ . . . 1 each
Hardwood Stock, ¾″ × 4″ × 25″ . . . . . . 1 each
Hardwood Dowel, ⅜″ diameter . . . . 5″
Hardwood Dowel, ¼″ diameter . . . . 2″
Hardwood Dowel, ⅛″ diameter . . . . 10″
Hardwood Toy Wheel, 1¼″ diameter . . 1 each
Carpenter's Glue . . . . small container

Cutting List
Part 1 . . . Fuselage . . . . Make 1
Part 2 . . . Right Wing Half . . . . Make 1
Part 3 . . . Left Wing Half . . . . Make 1
Part 4 . . . Horizontal Stabilizer Half Make 2
Part 5 . . . Vertical Stabilizer . . . . Make 1
Part 6 . . . Landing Gear Fairing . . . . . Make 2
Part 7 . . . Engine Cowling . . . . Make 1
Part 8 . . . Propeller . . . . Make 1

Instructions
LAYOUT
1. Lay out the fuselage (Part 1) on the hardwood block (Illus. 20.2).
2. Lay out Parts 2 through 7 on the ¾″ hardwood stock (Illus. 20.2 and 20.3). The wings (Parts 2 and 3) and the horizontal

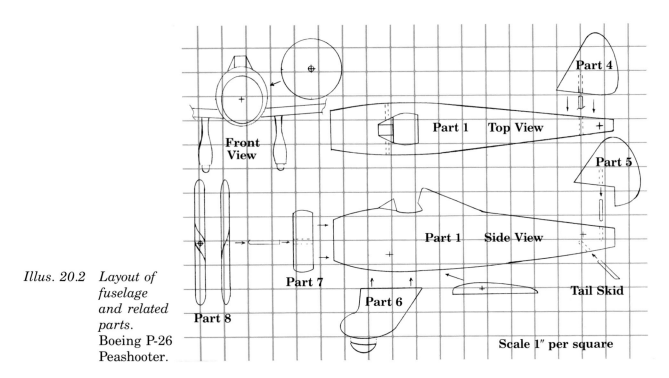

Illus. 20.2 Layout of fuselage and related parts. Boeing P-26 Peashooter.

Front View

Part 1   Top View

Part 4

Part 5

Part 1   Side View

Tail Skid

Part 7

Part 6

Part 8

Scale 1″ per square

stabilizer halves (Parts 4) should be laid out only once on the stock: cut the single piece to the basic shape with a band saw, and then rip into the two thinner parts. All of the tail stabilizers (Parts 4 and 5) should be ripped to a thickness of approximately ¼″. (The thickness of each remaining part is indicated in Illus. 20.2 and 20.3).

3. The engine cowling (Part 7) is essentially a 2½″-diameter circle, and can be cut out using a 2½″ hole saw on a drill press (Illus. 20.2).

4. Cut each of the parts to shape with your band saw.

5. Use a bench-mounted belt sander to form and shape the pieces as required (Illus. 20.4).

ASSEMBLY

6. Mark all of the drilling points on the parts as indicated in Illus. 20.2 and 20.3. Each of the holes is to be ⁵⁄₃₂″ in diameter. **NOTE:** Not all of the holes are to be drilled completely through the part.

7. Glue the wing halves (Parts 2 and 3) to each side of the fuselage (Part 1) by inser-

ting a 4″ long, ⅛″-diameter guide pin through the hole prepared in the fuselage and pressing the wing halves onto the guide pin until they butt firmly against the fuselage. Position them so that they are properly aligned as if one piece, parallel to the midline of the fuselage, and tilt each wingtip upwards so that it is approximately ½″ higher than the base of the wing (Illus. 20.2).

8. Install the horizontal stabilizer halves (Parts 4) in a similar manner using a 2″ guide pin. Position these parts level with the midline through the fuselage (Illus. 20.2).

9. The vertical stabilizer (Part 5) can now be installed in the same way with a 1″ guide pin. Position the vertical stabilizer perpendicular to the horizontal stabilizer and in line with the midline of the fuselage (Illus. 20.2).

10. Install the landing gear fairings (Parts 6) by gluing them to the underside of the wing at the locations shown by the dashed lines in Illus. 20.3.

11. Cut two semicircular pieces off of a 1¼″-diameter hardwood toy wheel, and glue

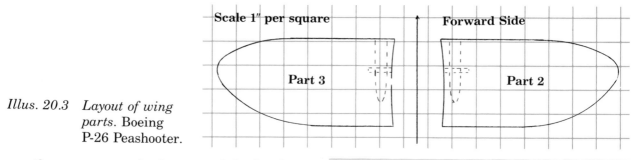

Scale 1″ per square | Forward Side

Part 3 | Part 2

Illus. 20.3 Layout of wing parts. Boeing P-26 Peashooter.

these parts to the bottom of the landing gear fairings (Parts 6) as shown in Illus. 20.2, side view.

12. Install a 1″ section of ⅛″ dowel for the tail skid as indicated in Illus. 20.2, side view.
13. Glue the engine cowling (Part 7) in place on the nose of the fuselage (Illus. 20.2).
14. Make the propeller drive shaft by cutting a 1½″ section of ¼″ dowel. Glue this shaft into the hole in the engine cowling so that it extends by ⅝″ (Illus. 20.2)
15. Make a 5″ long propeller from ⅜″ dowel by following the directions in Step 4 of Project 2 (page 10). Glue the propeller in place on the drive shaft (Illus. 20.2).
16. Your *Boeing P-26 Peashooter* is now complete. All that remains is finishing. It may be finished to preserve the natural

Illus. 20.4 Cut parts to shape on a band saw. Finish the shaping process by sanding each part as required on a bench-mounted belt sander.

wood look or painted in authentic colors to add a sense of realism to the display.
17. You may display your aircraft freestanding or mounted on a desk plaque.

Consolidated PBY-5A Catalina

Project 21

Illus. 21.1

The *PBY-5A Catalina* was a fast-flying amphibian aircraft powered by twin fourteen-cylinder radial engines to speeds approaching 200 mph (Illus. 21.1). It was built in 1935 but enjoyed a long career well beyond the end of World War II.

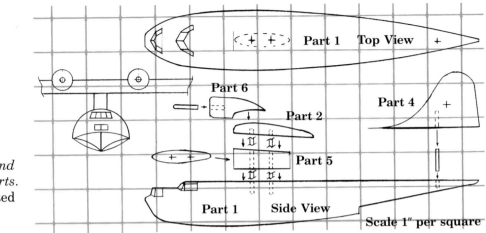

Illus. 21.2 Layout of fuselage and related parts. Consolidated PBY-5A Catalina.

Materials List

Hardwood Block, 1½″ × 1¾″ × 10″ . . . 1 each
Hardwood Stock, ¾″ × 4″ × 16″ . . . . . . 1 each
Hardwood Dowel, ⅝″ diameter . . . . 6″
Hardwood Dowel, ⅛″ diameter . . . . 6″
Carpenter's Glue . . . . small container

Cutting List

Part 1 . . . Fuselage . . . . Make 1
Part 2 . . . Wing . . . . Make 1
Part 3 . . . Horizontal Stabilizer Half Make 2
Part 4 . . . Vertical Stabilizer . . . . Make 1
Part 5 . . . Wing Support Pylon . . . . . . Make 1
Part 6 . . . Engine Cowling . . . . Make 2

Instructions

LAYOUT

1. Lay out the fuselage (Part 1) on the hard-wood block (Illus. 21.2).
2. Lay out Parts 2 through 5 on the ¾″ hardwood stock (Illus. 21.2 and 21.3).
   NOTE: These parts do not require the full ¾″ thickness and must be ripped to the proper thickness as shown in Illus. 21.2 and 21.3. However the thickness for the horizontal stabilizer halves and the vertical stabilizer (Parts 3 and 4) is not shown and should be ³⁄₁₆″.
3. The engine cowlings (Parts 6) are made from ⅝″-diameter dowel.
4. Cut all of these parts to their basic shape on your band saw.

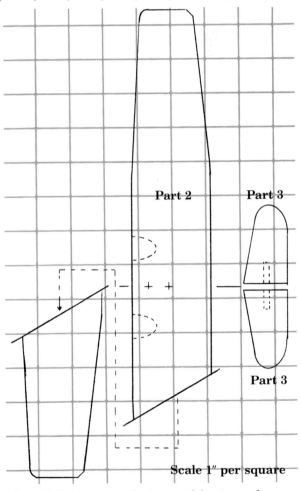

Illus. 21.3 Layout of wing and horizontal stabilizer. Consolidated PBY-5A Catalina.

5. Use a bench-mounted belt sander to form and shape the parts to their finished shapes as required (Illus. 21.4).

ASSEMBLY

6. Mark all of the drilling points on these parts as shown in Illus. 21.2 and 21.3. Each of these holes is to be ⁵⁄₃₂" in diameter.

   NOTE: Not all of the holes are to be drilled completely through the parts.

7. Install the wing (Part 2) and the wing support pylon (Part 5) in one operation by using two 1" guide pins made from ⅛" dowel (Illus. 21.2). Glue these parts together as shown and mount them on top of the fuselage (Part 1). Align the wing so that it is level and perpendicular to the fuselage.

8. Install the vertical stabilizer (Part 4) using a guide pin made from ⅛" dowel ¾" long (Illus. 21.2).

9. Glue the horizontal stabilizer halves (Parts 3) to the sides of the vertical stabilizer using a 1" guide pin made from ⅛" dowel to join them. Pass the guide pin through the hole in the vertical stabilizer and press the horizontal stabilizer halves firmly together. Set these stabilizers level with respect to the rest of the project.

10. Mount the engine cowlings (Parts 6) by gluing them to the top of the wing (Part 2) at the locations indicated by dashed lines in Illus. 21.3.

11. Cut the propeller drive shafts to ½" lengths from ⅛" dowel. Glue them into the holes at the front of the engine cowlings (Illus. 21.2, side view). No propellers have been designed since the amphibian aircraft is best displayed in flying mode and such small propellers are quite difficult to work with.

12. This completes your *Consolidated PBY-5A Catalina* except for finishing (Illus. 21.5). You can paint the aircraft with authentic colors to add a sense of realism to the display, or you can preserve the natural

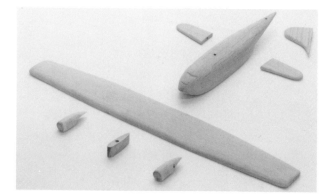

Illus. 21.4   Cut each part to basic shape on a band saw. Finish shaping by sanding as required on a bench-mounted belt sander.

Illus. 21.5   Fully assembled Consolidated PBY-5A Catalina *displayed in a flying attitude on a stand.*

wood finish to show the quality of the wood and your workmanship.

13. The *Consolidated PBY-5A Catalina* is best displayed on a stand in a flying position. A small brass nameplate on the base of the stand adds an elegant touch to the display.

Grumman J2F Duck

Illus. 22.1

The *Grumman J2F Duck* was first built in 1933 (Illus. 22.1). In spite of its ungainly look, the *Duck* served the Navy well for many years to come. The U.S. Navy used the *Duck* as an observation aircraft and for carrier-to-shore links as well as the air wings for noncarrier-type ships. It was a powerful airplane, but because of the massive float under the fuselage, it was not as agile as some of its contemporaries.

Materials List

Hardwood Block, 1½″ × 2″ × 9″ . . . . . 2 each
Hardwood Stock, ¾″ × 4″ × 14″ . . . . . . 1 each
Hardwood Dowel, ¼″ diameter . . . . 6″
Hardwood Dowel, ⅛″ diameter . . . . 16″
Hardwood Toy Wheels, ¾″ diameter . . . 2 each
Carpenter's Glue . . . . small container

Cutting List

Part 1 . . . Fuselage . . . . Make 1
Part 2 . . . Float . . . . Make 1
Part 3 . . . Lower Wing, right . . . . Make 1
Part 4 . . . Lower Wing, left . . . . Make 1
Part 5 . . . Upper Wing . . . . Make 1
Part 6 . . . Horizontal Stabilizer. Half . . . Make 2
Part 7 . . . Vertical Stabilizer . . . . Make 1
Part 8 . . . Propeller . . . . Make 1

Instructions

LAYOUT

1. Lay out the fuselage (Part 1) and the float (Part 2) on the hardwood block (Illus. 22.2 and 22.3).

2. Lay out Parts 3 through 7 on the ¾″ hardwood stock (Illus. 22.2 and 22.4).

   NOTE: These parts do not require the full ¾″ thickness and must be ripped to the proper thicknesses. The horizontal stabilizer halves and the vertical stabilizer (Parts 6 and 7) are to be ³⁄₁₆″ thick; the other parts have the thickness indicated in Illus. 22.2 and 22.4.

3. Cut all of the above parts to their basic shapes on a band saw.

4. Use a bench-mounted belt sander to form and shape each part as required (Illus. 22.5).

ASSEMBLY

5. Mark each of the drilling points on these parts as shown in Illus. 22.2, 22.3, and 22.4. The holes are to be drilled with a ⁵⁄₃₂″ bit with the exception of the propeller drive shaft mounting hole in the nose of the fuselage (Part 1) which is to be ⁹⁄₃₂″, and the engine counter set—also in the nose—and the wheel wells in the sides of

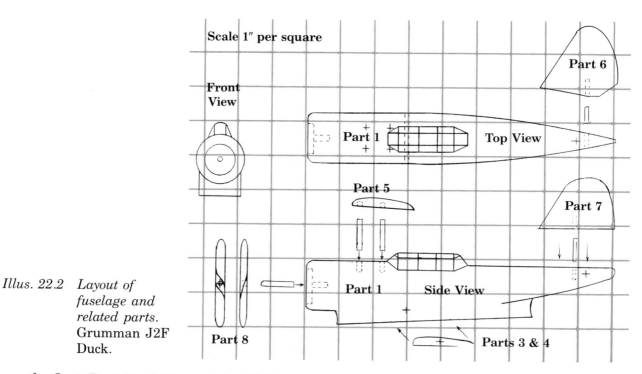

Scale 1" per square

Front View

Top View

Part 6

Part 1

Part 5

Part 7

Part 1   Side View

Part 8   Parts 3 & 4

Illus. 22.2   Layout of fuselage and related parts. Grumman J2F Duck.

the float (Part 2) which are to be ⅞" diameter. The three ⅞"-diameter holes are to be counter set to a depth of ³⁄₁₆".

6. Drill all of the holes at this time.

7. Position the float (Part 2) beneath the fuselage (Part 1), and glue in place.

8. Install the lower wing halves (Parts 3 and 4) using a ⅛" dowel guide pin cut to a 2½" length. Pass the guide pin through the hole prepared, and press the wing halves onto the pin so that they butt firmly against the fuselage. Position the wing halves as one piece and so that they are level with respect to the fuselage (Illus. 22.2).

9. Install the horizontal stabilizer halves in the same way using a ⅛" dowel guide pin cut to a 1¼" length (Illus. 22.2).

10. Install the vertical stabilizer in the same way using a ⅛" dowel guide pin cut to a length of ¾" (Illus. 22.2).

11. Cut four sections of ⅛" dowel to 1" lengths for the upper wing-to-fuselage support struts.

12. Glue these struts into the holes prepared at the top front of the fuselage, and allow them to extend uniformly to ¾".

13. Install the upper wing (Part 5) by aligning these struts with the holes previously drilled in the underside of the wing. Glue the upper wing on the struts so that the wing is parallel with the lower wing and perpendicular to the midline of the fuselage.

14. Cut four wing-to-wing support struts from ⅛" dowel to lengths of 2" each.

15. Glue the wing-to-wing struts in place by aligning them with the corresponding holes drilled towards each wingtip. The struts are to tilt forward at approximately 25°; so they will not actually engage with the holes but rather use them simply as glue sockets.

16. Cut the propeller shaft from a ¼"-diameter dowel to a length of 1". Glue it into the hole in the nose of the fuselage at this time (Illus. 22.2).

17. Make the propeller (Part 8) 3" long from ¼" dowel following the directions in Step 4 of Project 2 (page 10).

    NOTE: If you would like to display your aircraft in the flying mode, you may want to leave off the propeller to give the allusion of a spinning propeller.

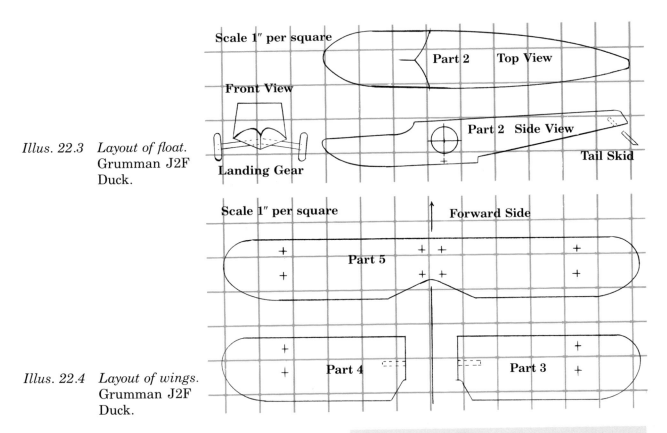

Scale 1″ per square

Front View

Part 2　Top View

Part 2　Side View

Tail Skid

Landing Gear

Illus. 22.3　Layout of float.
Grumman J2F
Duck.

Scale 1″ per square

Forward Side

Part 5

Part 4

Part 3

Illus. 22.4　Layout of wings.
Grumman J2F
Duck.

18. If you choose to install the propeller, glue it to the drive shaft at this time (Illus. 22.2).

19. If you plan to display the aircraft in the flying mode you may omit Steps 20 and 21, and simply glue the ¾″-diameter hardwood toy wheels into the wheel wells. Insert a piece of ⅛″ dowel into the axle hole of each wheel to give the appearance of an axle.

20. Cut the landing gear struts from ⅛″ dowel to a length of 1¼″. Glue them into the holes prepared in the float. Glue ¾″-diameter hardwood toy wheels to the ends of the landing gear struts (Illus. 22.3, front view).

21. Glue a ¾″ section of ⅛″ dowel into the hole prepared for the tail skid (Illus. 22.3).

22. Your *Grumman J2F Duck* is now complete except for finishing. You can paint the aircraft with authentic colors or preserve its natural wood finish.

Illus. 22.5　Cut each part to the basic shape
on a band saw. Finish shaping by
sanding as required on a bench-
mounted belt sander.

24. You may display this model freestanding or on a desk plaque if the landing gear has been installed. Or you may prefer displaying the aircraft on a flying stand if the landing gear is in the retracted position or the propeller is omitted.

Swordfish

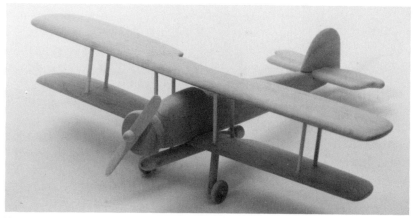

Illus. 23.1

The *Swordfish* was built in 1933 (Illus. 23.1). It was a strange looking, Allied torpedo bomber that survived until after World War II. It is duly famed for having destroyed more enemy ships than any other torpedo bomber airplane.

Materials List

Hardwood Block, 1¼″ × 1¾″ × 10″ . . . 1 each
Hardwood Stock, ¾″ × 4″ × 20″ . . . . . . 1 each
Hardwood Dowel, ⅜″ diameter . . . . 4″
Hardwood Dowel, ⁷⁄₁₆″ diameter . . . . 5″
Hardwood Dowel, ¼″ diameter . . . . 5″
Hardwood Dowel, ⅛″ diameter . . . . 25″
Hardwood Toy Wheels, ¾″ diameter . . . 2 each
Carpenter's Glue . . . . small container

Cutting List

Part 1 . . . Fuselage . . . . Make 1
Part 2 . . . Lower Wing . . . . Make 1
Part 3 . . . Upper Wing . . . . Make 1
Part 4 . . . Horizontal Stabilizer . . . . . . Make 1
Part 5 . . . Vertical Stabilizer . . . . Make 1
Part 6 . . . Engine Cowling . . . . Make 1
Part 7 . . . Propeller . . . . Make 1

Instructions

LAYOUT

1. Lay out the fuselage (Part 1) on the hardwood block (Illus. 23.2).
2. Lay out Parts 2 through 6 on the ¾″ stock (Illus. 23.2 and 23.3).

NOTE: These parts do not require the full ¾″ thickness and must be ripped to the proper thickness. The horizontal and vertical stabilizers (Parts 4 and 5) are to be ³⁄₁₆″ thick. The other parts have the proper thickness indicated in Illus. 23.2 and 23.3.

3. Use your band saw to cut these parts to shape. The engine cowling (Part 6) can be cut out with a 1½″ hole saw (Illus. 23.2).
4. Use a bench-mounted belt sander to form and shape each part to the finished shape required (Illus. 23.4).

ASSEMBLY

5. Mark all of the drilling points on the above parts as shown in Illus. 23.2 and 23.3. These holes are to be ⁵⁄₃₂″ diameter with the exception of the landing gear strut mounting holes on the underside of the wing which are to be ⁹⁄₃₂″.
6. Drill all of these holes at this time.
   NOTE: Many of the holes are not to be drilled completely through the parts.
7. Position the lower wing (Part 2) in the notch on the underside of the fuselage

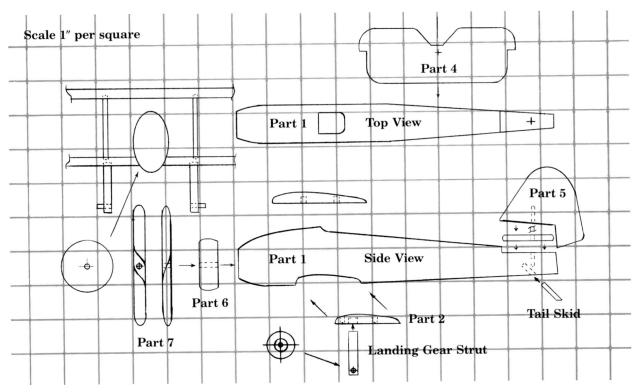

Part 4

Part 1   Top View

Part 5

Part 1   Side View

Part 6

Tail Skid

Part 7

Part 2

Landing Gear Strut

Illus. 23.2   Layout of fuselage and related parts. Swordfish.

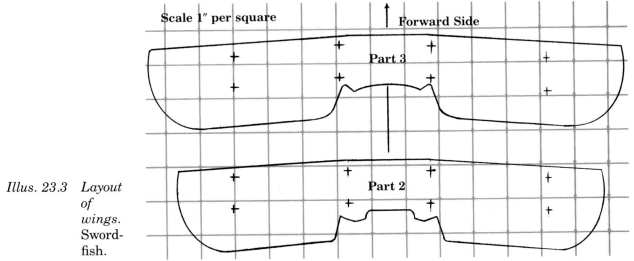

Scale 1″ per square   Forward Side

Part 3

Part 2

*Illus. 23.3   Layout
of
wings.
Sword-
fish.*

(Part 1), and secure it in place with carpenter's glue and two ¾″ wire brads.
Align the wing properly with respect to
the fuselage (Illus. 23.2).

8. Cut eight wing-to-wing support struts
from ⅛″ dowel at a length of 2″.

9. Glue these struts into the holes prepared
in the upper surface of the lower wing.

10. Now install the upper wing (Part 3) by

aligning each of the wing-to-wing support struts with the corresponding holes
on the underside of the upper wing. Make
sure that the upper wing is in the correct
position with respect to the lower wing
and the fuselage. The wing-to-wing
struts towards the outer ends of the
wings should be perpendicular to the
wings, while the ones towards the inner

side of the wings should tilt forward approximately 10°.

11. Glue the horizontal stabilizer (Part 4) in place in the notch provided. Position the horizontal stabilizer properly with respect to the fuselage and the wing assembly (Illus. 23.2, 23.4, and 23.5).

12. Use a ¾″ length of ⅛″ dowel as a guide pin to install the vertical stabilizer (Part 5). Make sure that this part is aligned perpendicular to the horizontal stabilizer (Illus. 23.2).

13. Position the engine cowling (Part 6) onto the nose of the fuselage and glue in place (Illus. 23.2).

14. Make a propeller drive shaft from a ¾″ length of ⅛″ dowel and glue it into the hole in the engine cowling. Allow it to extend from the cowling by ⅜″ (Illus. 23.2).

15. Make the propeller from a 3½″ length of ⅜″ dowel by following the directions in Step 4 of Project 2 (page 10).

16. Glue the completed propeller in place on the drive shaft (Illus. 23.2).

17. Make the landing gear struts from two 1⅝″ lengths of ¼″ dowel, each with a 5⁄32″ hole drilled ¼″ from one end.

18. Glue the landing gear struts into holes on the underside of the lower wing (Part 2) as shown in Illus. 23.2, side view. Set them perpendicular to the bottom of the wing.

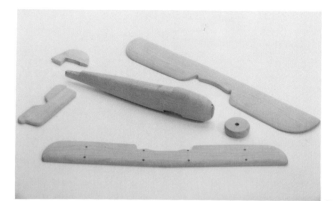

Illus. 23.4   Cut each part to shape on a band saw. Finish shaping by sanding as required on a bench-mounted belt sander.

19. Glue a ½″ length of ⅛″ dowel into each of the holes in the lower end of the landing gear struts. These dowels are the axles for the landing gear. Make sure the axles point outward towards the wingtips (Illus. 23.5).

20. Glue a ¾″-diameter hardwood toy wheel to each of the axles.

21. This completes your *Swordfish* except for finishing and adding a torpedo like that shown in Illus. 23.5. The model may be finished with a natural wood finish or painted with authentic colors to give a sense of realism to the aircraft.

22. It can be displayed freestanding or mounted on a desk plaque.

Illus. 23.5   Fully assembled Swordfish *with torpedo beneath.*

B-17
Flying Fortress

Illus. 24.1

Boeing's *B-17 Flying Fortress* was one of the most heavily armed bomber aircraft known at that time (Illus. 24.1). It was fitted with twelve guns that covered in all directions to protect the aircraft. The B-17 could carry up to 12,800 lbs. of bombs and was a stable high-altitude bombing platform. It was one of the first truly great large planes.

Materials List
Hardwood Block, 1¼" × 1½" × 14" . . . 1 each
Hardwood Stock, ¾" × 4" × 12" . . . . . . 1 each
Hardwood Dowel, ⅞" diameter . . . . 12"
Hardwood Dowel, ⅛" diameter . . . . 16"
Hardwood Screw Buttons, ½" diameter 2 each
Hardwood Toy Wheels, ¾" diameter . . . 2 each
Carpenter's Glue . . . . small container

Cutting List
Part 1 . . . Fuselage . . . . Make 1
Part 2 . . . Right Wing Half . . . . Make 1
Part 3 . . . Left Wing Half . . . . Make 1
Part 4 . . . Horizontal Stabilizer Half Make 2
Part 5 . . . Vertical Stabilizer Half . . . . Make 1
Part 6 . . . Engine Cowling . . . . Make 4
Part 7 . . . Gun Turrets . . . . Make 2

Instructions

LAYOUT
1. Lay out the fuselage (Part 1) on the hardwood block (Illus. 24.2).
2. Lay out Parts 2 through 5 on the ¾" hardwood stock (Illus. 24.2 and 24.3). These parts do not require the full ¾" thickness and must be ripped to the proper thicknesses as indicated in Illus. 24.2 and 24.3. The horizontal stabilizer halves and the vertical stabilizer (Parts 4 and 5) should be ³⁄₁₆" thick.
3. The engine cowlings (Parts 6) are to be made from ⅞"-diameter hardwood dowel. The wing notch must be cut out on a band saw or jigsaw and the other shaping done

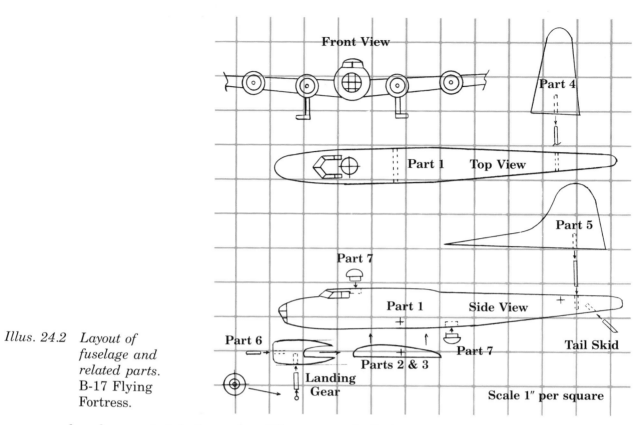

Front View

Part 4

Part 1   **Top View**

Part 5

Part 7

Part 1   **Side View**

*Illus. 24.2 Layout of
fuselage and
related parts.
B-17 Flying
Fortress.*

Part 6

Part 7   **Tail Skid**

Parts 2 & 3

**Landing
Gear**   **Scale 1″ per square**

on a bench-mounted belt sander (Illus. 24.2).

4. The gun turrets (Parts 7) are simply the ½″-diameter hardwood screw buttons.

5. Cut Parts 1 through 6 to their basic shape with your band saw or jigsaw.

6. Use a bench-mounted belt sander to form and shape all of these parts to their finished shapes (Illus. 24.4).

ASSEMBLY

7. Mark the drilling points on all of the above parts (Illus. 24.2 and 24.3). All of the holes are to be drilled with a ⁵⁄₃₂″ drill bit except for the two gun-turret mounting holes which should be drilled with a ½″ drill bit. The landing gear mounting holes should only be drilled in the two engine cowlings (Parts 6) that will become the inboard engines when installed. If you desire to display the model with the landing gear in the retracted position, do not drill these two holes.

NOTE: Many of the holes are not to be drilled completely through the parts.

8. The wing halves (Parts 2 and 3), the horizontal stabilizer halves (Parts 4), and the vertical stabilizer (Part 5) are to be installed using guide pins made from ⅛″ dowel sections. The length of these guide pins should be 3″, 2″, and 1″, respectively.

9. Install the two wing halves (Parts 2 and 3) by first passing the 3″ guide pin through the hole prepared for mounting the wing. Then glue the wing halves onto the guide pin and press them together until they butt firmly against the fuselage. Before the glue sets, tip the wingtips upwards so that they are 1″ higher than the base of each wing half (Illus. 24.2, front view).

10. Install the horizontal stabilizer halves (Parts 4) in the same way with the 2″ long guide pin. Set them level as one piece, parallel with the midline of the fuselage (Illus. 24.2, top view).

11. Install the vertical stabilizer, using the 1″ long guide pin. Set it perpendicular to the

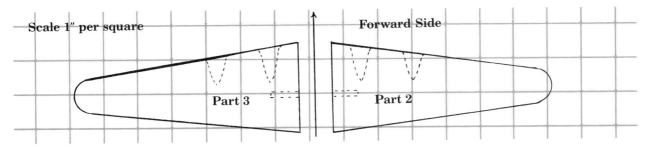

Part 3   Part 2

Illus. 24.3   Layout of wing with engine locations. B-17 Flying Fortress.

horizontal stabilizer (Illus. 24.2, side view).

12. Glue the gun turrets (Parts 7) into the ½″ holes in the top and underside of the fuselage (Illus. 24.2).

13. Fit the engine cowlings (Parts 6) to the locations indicated by the dashed lines on the forward side of the wing in Illus. 24.3. Make sure that they fit properly; use a small, half-round wood rasp to make any adjustments. After a proper fit is assured, glue them in place. Remember to place the two engine cowlings with the landing gear mounting holes at the inboard locations.

14. Cut four propeller drive shafts from ⅛″ dowel to a length of ½″. Round one end of these dowel sections with sandpaper (Illus. 24.2).

15. Glue the unrounded end of the propeller drive shafts into the holes at the front of the engine cowlings. Allow each to extend uniformly to a length of ¼″ (Illus. 24.2)

16. If you have decided to display the *B-17* with the landing gear retracted, omit the next five steps, and continue with Step 22.

17. Cut two landing gear struts from ⅛″ dowel to a length of ¾″.

18. Glue these struts into the holes prepared in the underside of the inboard engine cowlings. Allow them to extend from the cowlings by ½″ (Illus. 24.2, front view).

19. Cut two ⅛″ dowel sections for the landing gear axles to a length of ⅜″ long. Glue

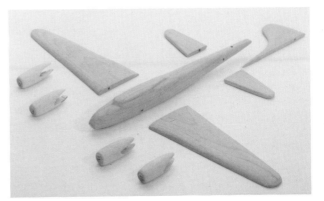

Illus. 24.4   Cut each part to shape on a band saw or jigsaw. Sand the parts to their finished form using a bench-mounted belt sander.

them to the ends of the landing gear struts as shown in the front view of Illus. 24.2.

20. Glue a ¾″-diameter hardwood toy wheel to each of the landing gear axles (Illus. 24.2).

21. Install a ¾″ length of ⅛″ dowel in the hole prepared for the tail skid. Allow it to extend ⅜″ (Illus. 24.2).

22. Your *B-17 Flying Fortress* is now complete except for finishing. You may preserve its natural wood finish or paint the aircraft in authentic colors and markings to add a sense of realism.

23. With the landing gear installed, the aircraft may be left freestanding or mounted on a desk plaque. If the landing gear has been omitted, then the aircraft must be displayed in a flying attitude on a stand.

Douglas C-47 Skytrain

Illus. 25.1

The *Douglas C-47 Skytrain*, also known as the *DC-3 Dakota*, has become the most widely used air transport in the history of aviation (Illus. 25.1). The *C-47 Skytrain* was originally built in 1935, yet many of these airplanes are still in use today. It has been used for many purposes—both military and civilian—as commercial airliner, paratroop carrier, cargo transport, and even gun ship. It has proven to be a durable workhorse.

Materials List

Hardwood Block, 1¼″ × 1½″ × 10″ . . . 1 each
Hardwood Stock, ¾″ × 4″ × 7″ . . . . 1 each
Hardwood Dowel, ⅞″ diameter . . . . 6″
Hardwood Dowel, ⅛″ diameter . . . . 18″
Hardwood Toy Wheels, ¾″ diameter . . . 2 each
Carpenter's Glue . . . . small container

Cutting List

Part 1 . . . Fuselage . . . . Make 1
Part 2 . . . Right Wing Half . . . . Make 1
Part 3 . . . Left Wing Half . . . . Make 1
Part 4 . . . Horizontal Stabilizer Half Make 2
Part 5 . . . Vertical Stabilizer . . . . Make 1
Part 6 . . . Engine Cowling . . . . Make 2

Instructions

LAYOUT

1. Lay out the fuselage (Part 1) on the hardwood block (Illus. 25.2).

2. Lay out Parts 2 through 5 on the ¾″ hardwood stock (Illus. 25.2 and 25.3).
   NOTE: These parts do not require the full ¾″ thickness and must be ripped to the proper thickness. The horizontal stabilizer halves and the vertical stabilizer (Parts 4 and 5) are to be ³⁄₁₆″ thick; this is not shown in the illustrations.

3. The two engine cowlings (Parts 6) are to be made from ⅞″-diameter hardwood dowel by first cutting out the wing mounting notch and then shaping the contour on a bench-mounted belt sander.

4. Parts 1 through 6 should now be cut to their basic shapes on a band saw or jigsaw.

5. Use the bench-mounted belt sander to form and shape each of these parts to their finished shapes (Illus. 25.4).

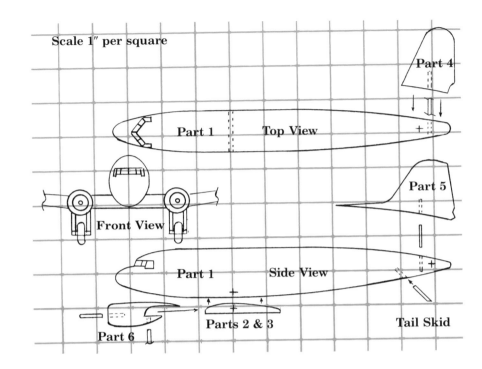

Scale 1″ per square

Part 1   Top View

Part 4

Front View

Part 5

Part 1   Side View

Parts 2 & 3

Part 6

Tail Skid

Illus. 25.2   Layout of fuselage and related parts. Douglas C-47 Skytrain.

ASSEMBLY

6. Mark each of the drilling points on all of the above parts. These holes are all to be drilled with a ⁵⁄₃₂″ drill bit.
   NOTE: many of the holes are not to be drilled completely through the parts (Illus. 25.2 and 25.3).

7. Several guide pins made from ⅛″ dowel will be used to install the wing halves (Parts 2 and 3), the horizontal stabilizer halves (Parts 4), and the vertical stabilizer (Part 5). Cut these guide pins to lengths of 3″, 1½″, and ¾″, respectively.

8. Install the wing halves (Parts 2 and 3) by first passing the 3″ guide pin through the hole prepared in the fuselage (Part 1). Then apply glue and press the wing halves onto the guide pin until they butt firmly against the sides of the fuselage (Illus. 25.2).

9. Raise the wingtips upwards until they are approximately ½″ higher than the base of the wing halves.

10. Install the horizontal stabilizer halves in the same way, using the 1½″ guide pin. Set them as one piece, level with respect to the rest of the aircraft (Illus. 25.2).

11. Glue the vertical stabilizer in place using the ¾″ guide pin. Set it perpendicular to the horizontal stabilizer and in line with the midline of the fuselage (Illus. 25.2).

12. Glue the engine cowlings (Parts 6) into place. The dashed lines in Illus. 25.3 show the engine mounting locations.

13. Cut two ½″ lengths of ⅛″ dowel for propeller shafts. Glue the propeller shafts into the holes in the front of the engine cowlings (Illus. 25.2).

14. If you choose to display your *C-47* with the landing gear in the retracted position, omit the following four steps and resume with Step 19.

15. Cut four landing gear struts from ⅛″ dowel to a length of ¾″ (Illus. 25.2).

16. Glue these struts into holes prepared in the bottom of the engine cowlings.

17. Make two ½″ long axles from ⅛″ dowel. Insert each through the hole in a ¾″-diameter hardwood wheel, and then glue these wheel axle assemblies to the bottom of the landing gear struts (Illus. 25.2, front view).

18. Make a tail skid from ⅛″ dowel cut to a ¾″ length. Install the tail skid with car-

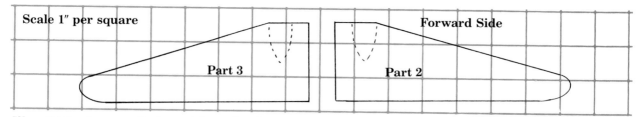

Forward Side

Part 3

Part 2

Illus. 25.3   Layout of wing with engine locations. Douglas C-47 Skytrain.

penter's glue as shown in Illus. 25.2, side view.

19. Your *DC-3 Dakota*—the *Douglas C-47 Skytrain*—is now complete and ready to finish. It may be painted with authentic colors to give a sense of realism, or you can preserve the natural wood finish to show the quality of the wood and your workmanship.

20. Display the aircraft freestanding or mounted on a desk plaque if the landing gear was installed. Without the landing gear, you will need a stand to display the model in a flying attitude.

Illus. 25.4   Cut each part to shape on a band saw or jigsaw. Finish shaping by sanding as required on a bench-mounted belt sander.

Vought SB2U Vindicator

Project 26

Illus. 26.1

The *Vought SB2U Vindicator* was a powerful U.S. Navy dive-bomber built in 1936 specifically for carrier-based operations (Illus. 26.1). The construction of this model has some options that you may find challenging. The wings can actually fold upward, the landing gear can retract, and the canopy hatches can slide open. These options are design ideas that you may choose to include in your construction.

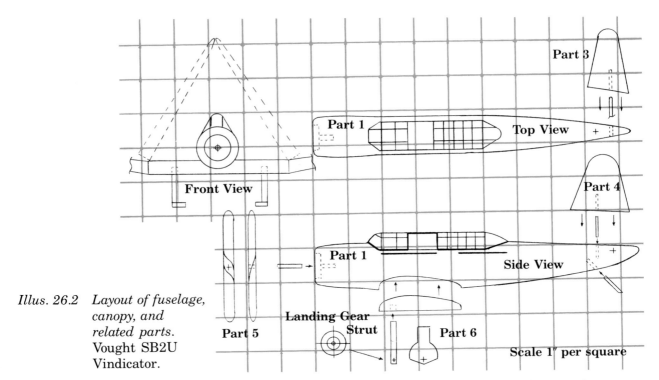

Illus. 26.2 *Layout of fuselage, canopy, and related parts. Vought SB2U Vindicator.*

Front View

Part 1 **Top View**

Part 3

Part 4

Part 1 **Side View**

Landing Gear Strut

Part 5 **Part 6**

Scale 1″ per square

Materials List

Hardwood Block, $1\frac{1}{4}$″ × $1\frac{3}{4}$″ × 9″ . . . . 1 each
Hardwood Stock, $\frac{3}{4}$″ × 4″ × 15″ . . . . . . 1 each
Hardwood Dowel, $\frac{1}{4}$″ diameter . . . . 6″
Hardwood Dowel, $\frac{3}{16}$″ diameter . . . . 4″
Hardwood Dowel, $\frac{1}{8}$″ diameter . . . . 6″
Butt Hinges, $\frac{5}{8}$″ . . . . 2 each*
Hinge Point Model Hinges . . . . 2 each*
Brass Rod, $\frac{1}{16}$″ diameter . . . . 36″*
Hardwood Toy Wheels, $\frac{3}{4}$″ diameter . . . 2 each
Carpenter's Glue . . . . small container
Epoxy Glue . . . . small amount*
Required for design options.

Cutting List

Part 1 . . . Fuselage . . . . Make 1
Part 2 . . . Wing . . . . Make 1
Part 3 . . . Horizontal Stabilizer Half Make 2
Part 4 . . . Vertical Stabilizer . . . . Make 1
Part 5 . . . Propeller . . . . Make 1
Part 6 . . . Landing Gear Doors . . . . . . Make 2

Instructions

LAYOUT

1. Lay out the fuselage (Part 1) on the hardwood block (Illus. 26.2).

CANOPY OPTION: If you choose to make the sliding canopy, lay out the fuselage by following the bold lines running along the canopy area.

2. Lay out Parts 2 through 4 and Part 6 on the $\frac{3}{4}$″ hardwood stock. These parts are to be quite a bit thinner than the stock and must be ripped to the proper thickness. The horizontal stabilizer halves and the vertical stabilizer (Parts 3 and 4) are to be $\frac{3}{16}$″ thick; all other parts have the thickness indicated in Illus. 26.2 and 26.3.

3. Cut all of the above parts to their basic shapes with your band saw or jigsaw.

4. Use your bench-mounted belt sander to form and shape each of the parts to its finished shape as indicated in Illus. 26.2 and 26.3.

ASSEMBLY

5. Mark each of the drilling points on Parts 1 through 4. The recess in the nose of the fuselage (Part 1) is to be cut with a $\frac{3}{4}$″ center bore drill and counterset to a depth of $\frac{1}{8}$″. All the remaining holes are to be a $\frac{5}{32}$″ diameter (Illus. 26.2 and 26.3).

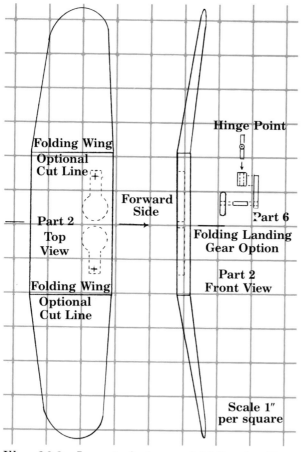

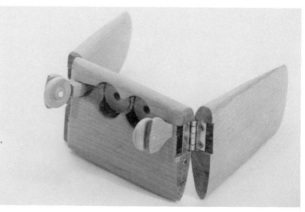

Illus. 26.4   *Landing gear assemblies installed with hinge point model hinges.*

Illus. 26.3   Layout of wing and folding landing gear. Vought SB2U Vindicator.

LANDING GEAR OPTION: If you choose to make the retractable landing gear, do not drill the holes in the wing for mounting the landing gear struts.

NOTE: Some of these holes are not to be drilled completely through the parts.

6. **FOLDING WING OPTION:** If you choose to make the folding wings, cut the wing (Part 2) into three sections along the optional cut lines (Illus. 26.3).

7. **RETRACTABLE LANDING GEAR OPTION:** Steps 7 through 15. Lay out the landing gear wells on the underside of the middle wing section (Illus. 26.3). Drill the two marked circles with a ⅞″ center bore drill to a depth of ⁵⁄₁₆″. Use a rotary carving tool to carve away the remaining area in the landing gear well also to a depth of ⁵⁄₁₆″ (Illus. 26.4).

8. Cut two axles from ⅛″ dowel to a length of ⅜″. Glue the axles in place in the hole that was prepared in the landing gear door (Part 6).

9. Glue the ¾″-diameter hardwood toy wheels onto the axles as shown (Illus. 26.3).

10. Make two landing gear mounting blocks from hardwood. These blocks are ¼″ × ¼″ × ⁵⁄₁₆″ (Illus. 26.3).

11. Glue these blocks in place on the landing gear doors as shown in Illus. 26.3.

12. Drill a ⅛″ hole through the landing gear mounting blocks from the top for installing the hinge (Illus. 26.3).

13. Drill a ⅛″ hole as indicated towards the outside of each landing gear well (Illus. 26.3, top view).

14. Install the landing gear using hinge point model hinges (Illus. 26.5) with epoxy glue sparingly to ensure proper retraction and extension (Illus. 26.4). These hinges are available at hobbie shops. The ends of the hinge points are longer than needed and must be cut to the proper length of approximately ⅜″. If the ends protrude through the top of the wing, they can be sanded smooth later.

15. Some adjustments may be required to allow the full closure of the landing gear doors. These can be made by careful sanding or filing after the epoxy has thoroughly cured.

Illus. 26.5   *Each hinge point model hinge will need to be cut to a required length of ³⁄₈".*

16. **FOLDING WING OPTION:** The folding wings can be made by simply installing a ⅝" butt hinge at each folding point (Illus. 26.4). Set the hinge so that it is on the thicker part of the wing, about ³⁄₈" behind the forward edge off the wing.

17. **SLIDING CANOPY OPTION:** Steps 17 through 23. Make the stationary portions of the canopy as shown in Illus. 26.6. This is done by using ¹⁄₁₆"-diameter brass rod, available at hobbie shops, and bending it into the various shapes of the canopy parts. The sections are then installed on the fuselage (Part 1) by drilling small holes at the required locations and inserting the ends of the brass canopy frame into these holes. Epoxy glue should be used for securing them in place. Solder the brass sections together at their intersecting points.

18. The sliding sections of the canopy will be mounted into small grooves on each side of the fuselage just below the cockpit area (Illus. 26.2 and 26.6). These grooves can be made with a rotary carving tool. They should be slightly wider than the ¹⁄₁₆"-diameter brass rod which will slide through them and approximately ¹⁄₁₆" deep as well.

19. The two end frames of the sliding canopy sections are shaped similar to the frame sections of the stationary portion but must be slightly larger so that they will slide over them without binding. The ends should be bent inward horizontally to face each other (Illus. 26.7).

20. Now cut the connecting brass sections to a ⅞" length and solder them in place as shown (Illus. 26.7).

21. Stretch the sliding canopy sections open

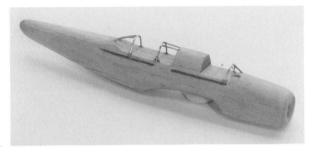

Illus. 26.6   *Stationary portions of the canopy installed on the fuselage.*

only enough to get the bent ends into the grooves for installation (Illus. 26.8)

22. Glass can be simulated by bubbling white glue between the various framework sections of the brass canopy and allowing it to dry there. This should not be done, however, until the finishing process has been completed. Some touch-up of the paint or finish may be required after white glue has been applied.

Illus. 26.7   *Sliding canopy sections must have the brass rod ends bent horizontally so that the rod can slide in the grooves prepared in the fuselage.*

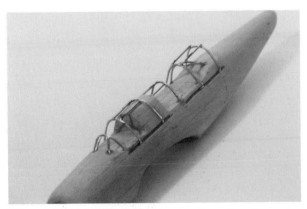

Illus. 26.8   *Sliding canopy sections in place.*

23. Install the wing (Part 2) to the fuselage (Part 1) by positioning it into the notch provided (Illus. 26.2). Secure it in place with carpenter's glue.

24. Install the horizontal stabilizer halves (Parts 3) using a ⅛″ dowel guide pin about 1¼″ long. Pass the guide pin through the prepared hole; press the stabilizer halves onto the guide pin and firmly against the sides of the fuselage. Set these parts level with respect to the rest of the aircraft (Illus. 26.2).

25. The vertical stabilizer (Part 4) can now be glued in place in the same manner using a ¾″-long guide pin. Position it perpendicular to the horizontal stabilizer and parallel with the midline of the fuselage (Illus. 26.2).

26. Glue a ¾″ length of ⅛″ dowel into the hole prepared for mounting the tail skid (Illus. 26.2, side view).

27. **NONRETRACTABLE LANDING GEAR OPTION:** Steps 27 through 32. If you have chosen not to construct the folding landing gear then you can install permanent landing gear as follows.

28. Drill the two 5⁄32″ holes into the underside of the wing at the locations indicated in Illus. 26.2, side and front views. Drill these holes to a depth of ⅛″.

29. Cut two ⅛″-dowel landing gear struts to ¾″ lengths and glue them into the holes just drilled.

30. Cut ⅛″ diameter axles to ⅜″ lengths and glue them across the bottom of the struts (Illus. 26.2, front view).

31. Glue the two ¾″-diameter hardwood toy wheels onto the axles.

32. Glue the landing gear doors (Parts 6) to the outboard side of the landing gear struts (Illus. 26.2).

33. Cut the propeller drive shaft from a 1″ length of 3⁄16″ dowel. Glue the shaft into the hole in the nose of the fuselage.

34. The propeller is made of ¼″ dowel cut to a length of 3″ following the directions given in Step 4 of Project 2 (page 10). Install the propeller on the drive shaft with carpenter's glue (Illus. 26.2).

    NOTE: The propeller can be omitted if you prefer displaying the aircraft in a flying attitude.

35. This completes the construction of your *Vought SB2U Vindicator*; it is ready for finishing (Illus. 26.9). It may be painted with authentic colors to give a sense of realism to the display or finished in a natural wood finish to show the quality of workmanship. If you choose the natural wood finish, the sliding canopy framework should, nevertheless, be painted with some complementary color to cover the solder joints.

36. You may display this model freestanding, mounted on a desk plaque, or in a flying attitude on a hardwood stand.

Illus. 26.9 Fully assembled Vought SB2U Vindicator with the propeller omitted for display in a flying attitude.

·8·
JUST PRIOR TO THE WAR

P-40 Warhawk

Illus. 27.1

The *P-40 Warhawk* is the Curtiss-built fighter that was flown for the Allies by the legendary "Flying Tigers" squadron during World War II (Illus. 27.1). It was flown by others as well—many others. In fact the *P-40* was the one fighter aircraft that saw action on every major front during that great conflict. It was fast, powerful, and tough.

Materials List
Hardwood Block, 1¼″ × 2″ × 9″ ..... *1 each*
Hardwood Stock, ¾″ × 4″ × 14″ ...... *1 each*
Hardwood Dowel, ⅛″ diameter .... *8″*
Hardwood Toy Wheels, ¾″ diameter ... *2 each*
Carpenter's Glue .... *small container*

Cutting List
Part 1 ... Fuselage .... *Make 1*
Part 2 ... Wing .... *Make 1*
Part 3 ... Horizontal Stabilizer Half Make 2
Part 4 ... Vertical Stabilizer .... *Make 1*

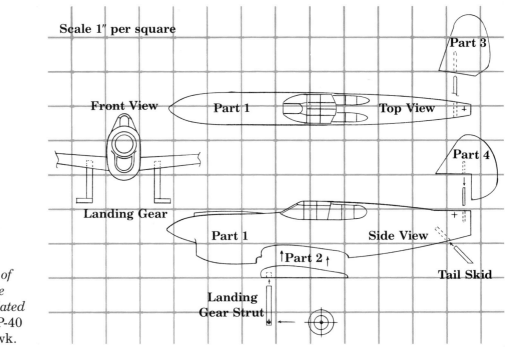

Illus. 27.2 Layout of fuselage and related parts. P-40 Warhawk.

Instructions

LAYOUT

1. Lay out the fuselage (Part 1) on the hardwood block (Illus. 27.2).

2. Lay out the wing (Part 2) on the ¾″ hardwood stock (Illus. 27.3).
   NOTE: The wing is to be cut with a dihedral angle so that the ends or tips reach upwards. This must be done while cutting the part sideways from the stock.

3. Lay out the horizontal stabilizer halves and the vertical stabilizer (Parts 3 and 4) on the ¾″ hardwood stock (Illus. 27.2). These parts are to be ripped to a thickness of ³⁄₁₆″.

4. Use your band saw or jigsaw to cut each of the above parts to shape.

5. Use bench-mounted belt sander to form and shape all of these parts to their finished shapes as required (Illus. 27.4).

ASSEMBLY

6. Mark all the drilling points on each of the parts (Illus. 27.2 and 27.3). All of these holes are to be a ⁵⁄₃₂″ diameter.

NOTE: Some of the holes are not to be drilled completely through the parts.
   Drill all of these holes at this time.

7. Position the wing (Part 2) in the notch prepared in the fuselage (Part 1). Secure it in place with carpenter's glue and two ¾″ wire brads (Illus. 27.2).

8. Install the horizontal stabilizer halves (Parts 3) using a ⅛″-diameter dowel guide pin cut to a ¾″ length and carpenter's glue. Pass the guide pin through the hole prepared at the rear of the fuselage; press the stabilizer halves onto the guide until they butt firmly against the sides of the fuselage (Illus. 27.2). Set these parts as one piece, level with respect to the rest of the aircraft.

9. Glue the vertical stabilizer (Part 4) in place using a ¾″ long guide pin cut from ⅛″ dowel. Align the vertical stabilizer perpendicular to the horizontal stabilizer and in line with the midline of the fuselage (Illus. 27.2).

10. If you would prefer displaying the *P-40* in a flying attitude with the wheels retracted, omit Steps 11 through 15.

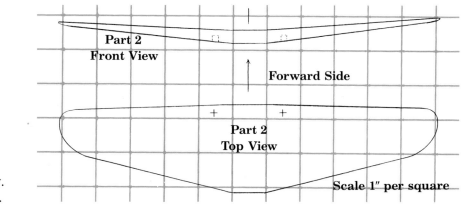

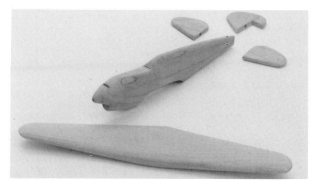

Illus. 27.3 Layout of wing.
P-40 Warhawk.

Part 2
Front View

Forward Side

Part 2
Top View

Scale 1″ per square

11. Cut two sections of ⅛″ dowel to a length of ⅞″ for the landing gear struts (Illus. 27.2).

12. Glue these struts into the holes in the underside of the wing (Illus. 27.2, side view). Align them to be perpendicular to the bottom of the wing, front to back, but parallel with each other when seen head-on (Illus. 27.2, front view).

13. Make the axles from ⅛″ dowel cut to be ⅜″ long. Glue them to the ends of the landing gear struts (Illus. 27.2, front view).

14. Glue a ¾″-diameter hardwood toy wheel to each landing gear axle.

15. Glue a ¾″ length of ⅛″ dowel into the tail skid mounting hole. Allow it to extend ⅜″ (Illus. 27.2, side view).

16. This completes your *P-40 Warhawk* except for finishing (Illus. 27.5). You can preserve the natural wood finish to show the

Illus. 27.4 Cut each part to shape on a band saw or jigsaw. Finish shaping by sanding as required on a bench-mounted belt sander.

quality of the wood and workmanship or paint the aircraft with authentic colors to add a sense of realism.

17. You may display the aircraft on a flying stand or mounted on a desk plaque depending on whether you chose to have the landing gear up or down.

Illus. 27.5 Fully assembled P-40 Warhawk in a flying attitude on a hardwood stand.

Ju 87 Stuka

Illus. 28.1

The *Ju 87 Stuka* was designed and built by the Axis powers primarily to deliver its payload of bombs from a vertical dive (Illus. 28.1). This was the most accurate method of dive-bombing. The *Stuka* had the power and strength to withstand this form of combat. However, it was not well suited for encountering other aircraft in aerial combat and suffered greatly during Allied fighter engagements.

Materials List

Hardwood Block, 1¼″ × 2½″ × 12″ . . . 1 each
Hardwood Stock, ¾″ × 4″ × 20″ . . . . . . 1 each
Hardwood Dowel, ⅛″ diameter . . . . 8″
Hardwood Toy Wheel, ¾″ diameter . . . . 1 each
Carpenter's Glue . . . . small container

Cutting List

Part 1 . . . Fuselage . . . . Make 1
Part 2 . . . Right Wing Half . . . . Make 1
Part 3 . . . Left Wing Half . . . . Make 1
Part 4 . . . Horizontal Stabilizer Half Make 2
Part 5 . . . Vertical Stabilizer . . . . Make 1
Part 6 . . . Wheel Spats . . . . Make 2

Instructions

LAYOUT

1. Lay out the fuselage (Part 1) on the hardwood block (Illus. 28.2).

2. Lay out the wing halves (Parts 2 and 3) on ¾″ hardwood stock (Illus. 28.3). These parts will have an "inverted gull wing" shape that will require cutting sideways through the material.

3. Lay out the horizontal stabilizer halves (Parts 4) and the vertical stabilizer (Part 5) on ¾″ hardwood stock that has been ripped to a ³⁄₁₆″ thickness (Illus. 28.2).

4. Lay out the wheel spats (Parts 6) on hardwood stock that has been ripped to a ⅜″ thickness (Illus. 28.2).

5. Use your band saw or jigsaw to cut all of the above parts to their basic shape.

6. Use bench-mounted belt sander to form and shape each part to the finished shape as required (Illus. 28.4).

ASSEMBLY

7. Mark each of the drilling points on these parts (Illus. 28.2 and 28.3). All of these

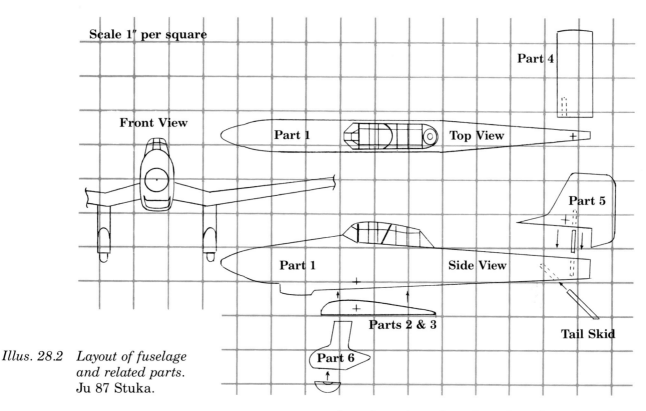

Scale 1″ per square

Front View

Part 1 · Top View

Part 4

Part 1 · Side View

Part 5

Parts 2 & 3

Tail Skid

Part 6

Illus. 28.2   Layout of fuselage and related parts. Ju 87 Stuka.

holes are to be drilled to a ⁵⁄₃₂″ diameter. **NOTE:** Some of the holes should not be drilled completely through the parts.

8. The wing halves (Parts 2 and 3), the horizontal stabilizer halves (Parts 4), and the vertical stabilizer (Part 5) will be installed using guide pins cut from ⅛″ dowel to 1¼″, 1½″ and ¾″ lengths, respectively. You will need two of the 1¼″ length guide pins to mount both wing halves.

9. Glue the wing halves (Parts 2 and 3) in position by placing the guide pins into the prepared holes in the wing halves and inserting them into the corresponding holes in the fuselage (Part 1). Press these parts together until the wing halves butt firmly against the sides of the fuselage. Position the wing halves as one piece and in proper alignment with the fuselage; raise the wingtips upwards until they are uniformly 1″ or so above your workbench with the aircraft assembly sitting flat on the bench (Illus. 28.2, front view, and 28.3).

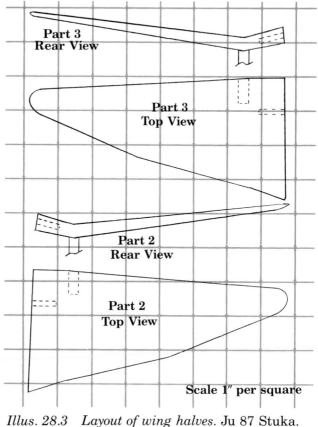

Part 3
Rear View

Part 3
Top View

Part 2
Rear View

Part 2
Top View

Scale 1″ per square

Illus. 28.3   Layout of wing halves. Ju 87 Stuka.

10. The horizontal stabilizer halves (Parts 4) are to be installed in a similar way using the 1½″ long guide pin. This time pass the guide pin through the hole in the rear of the fuselage, and press the parts onto it from each side. Again press them firmly against the sides of the fuselage (Illus. 28.2).

11. Glue the vertical stabilizer (Part 5) in place using the ¾″ long guide pin. Align it to be perpendicular to the horizontal stabilizer and parallel with the midline of the fuselage (Illus. 28.2).

12. The wheel spats (Parts 6) are to simply be glued to the underside of the wing at the locations indicated Illus. 28.2. Set them straight with respect to the rest of the project (Illus. 28.2, front view).

13. Take one ¾″-diameter hardwood toy wheel and cut off two sides of the tire and wheel keeping the outside parts; note the moon-shaped wheel part in Illus. 28.2, side view.

14. Glue these small wheel sections to the underside of the wheel spats. This creates the illusion of a complete wheel covered by the fendered area of the wheel spat (Illus. 28.2).

15. Make the tail skid from a ¾″ length of ⅛″

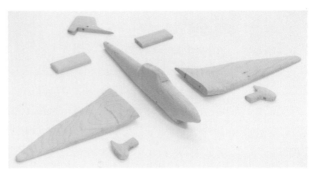

Illus. 28.4   Cut each part to shape on a band saw or jigsaw. Finish shaping by sanding as required on a bench-mounted belt sander.

dowel. Glue it into position at this time (Illus. 28.2).

16. The *Ju 87 Stuka* dive-bomber is now complete and ready for finishing (Illus. 28.5). You can paint the aircraft with authentic colors to add a sense of realism to its display or you may choose a natural wood finish to show the quality of the wood and your workmanship.

17. Displaying your *Stuka* can be as simple as placing it on a shelf as is or mounting it on a finely finished hardwood desk plaque. The addition of a small brass name plate to the plaque adds an elegant touch.

Illus. 28.5   Fully assembled Ju 87 Stuka.

Messerschmitt Bf 109

Illus. 29.1

The *Messerschmitt Bf 109* was Germany's finest fighter during the early part of World War II (Illus. 29.1). It had a powerful 1200 hp engine and could well contend with the Allied British fighters of that era in the dog fight. This aircraft of the Axis powers is credited with more victories in the air than any other fighter in the history of combat.

Materials List

Hardwood Block, 1⅝″ × 2½″ × 15″ . . . 1 each
Hardwood Stock, ¾″ × 4″ × 12″ . . . . . . 1 each
Hardwood Dowel, ¼″ diameter . . . . 6″
Hardwood Dowel, ⅛″ diameter . . . . 10″
Hardwood Toy Wheels, 1¼″ diameter 2 each
Carpenter's Glue . . . . small container

Cutting List

Part 1 . . . Fuselage . . . . Make 1
Part 2 . . . Wing Half . . . . Make 2
Part 3 . . . Horizontal Stabilizer Half Make 2
Part 4 . . . Vertical Stabilizer . . . . Make 1
Part 5 . . . Landing Gear Doors . . . . . Make 2

Instructions
LAYOUT

1. Lay out the fuselage (Part 1) on the hardwood block (Illus. 29.2).
2. Lay out the wing halves (Parts 2), the horizontal stabilizer halves (Parts 3), and the vertical stabilizer (Part 4) on the ¾″ hardwood stock (Illus. 29.2 and 29.3).

NOTE: These parts do not require the full ¾″ thickness and should be ripped to the proper thicknesses shown in Illus. 29.2 and 29.3. The horizontal stabilizer halves and the vertical stabilizer (Parts 3 and 4) are to be ³⁄₁₆″ thick, which isn't shown.

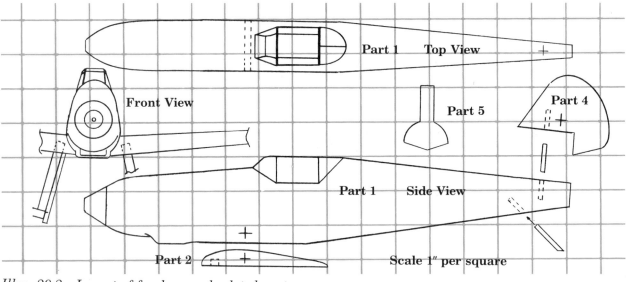

Illus. 29.2 *Layout of fuselage and related parts.* Messerschmitt Bf 109.

3. Use a band saw to cut all of the above parts to their basic shapes.

4. Now the finished shapes can be formed and shaped by using a bench-mounted belt sander (Illus. 29.4).

ASSEMBLY

5. Mark each of the drilling points on these parts (Illus. 29.2 and 29.3). The holes for mounting the landing gear struts are to be drilled to a $\frac{9}{32}''$ diameter. They should be omitted if you plan to display the aircraft in a flying mode. The other holes should be drilled to a $\frac{5}{32}''$ diameter.

   NOTE: Some of the holes should not be drilled completely through the parts.

6. The installation of the wing halves (Parts 2), the horizontal stabilizer halves (Parts 3), and the vertical stabilizer (Part 4) will be done using guide pins cut from $\frac{1}{8}''$ dowel to lengths of $3\frac{1}{2}''$, $1\frac{1}{2}''$, and $1''$ respectively.

7. Glue the wing halves (Parts 2) in place by passing the $3\frac{1}{2}''$ guide pin through the hole in the fuselage (Part 1) and pushing the wings onto it from each side. Press the wing firmly against the sides of the fuselage. With the fuselage sitting flat on your work bench the wingtips should be lifted upwards until they are $1\frac{1}{2}''$ above

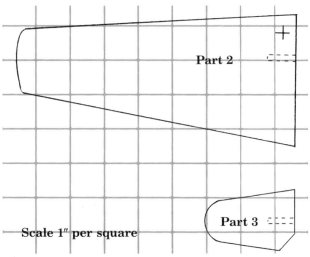

Illus. 29.3 *Layout wing and horizontal stabilizer parts.* Messerschmitt Bf 109.

the bench top. Allow the glue to set with the wings in this attitude (Illus. 29.2).

8. Install the vertical stabilizer (Part 4) using the $1''$ guide pin and carpenter's glue. Set it perpendicular to the rest of the project and parallel to the midline of the fuselage (Illus. 29.2).

9. Use the $1\frac{1}{2}''$ guide pin to install the horizontal stabilizer halves (Parts 3) with glue. This is to be done in the same manner used to install the wings. Position these parts level with respect to the rest of the aircraft and parallel to the midline of the fuselage.

10. If you prefer displaying your *Messerschmitt Bf 109* with the wheels retracted, omit Steps 11 through 14.

11. Cut two landing gear struts from ¼" dowel to lengths of 1½". Glue these struts into the holes in the underside of the wings (Illus. 29.2, front view).

12. Cut two ⅝" long axles from ¼" dowel, and glue them to the ends of the landing gear struts so that they point outward towards the wingtips.

13. Glue the landing gear doors (Parts 5) to the inside of the landing gear struts (Illus. 29.2).

14. Cut the tail skid from ⅛" dowel to a ¾" length. Glue it into the hole prepared towards the rear of the fuselage.

15. Your *Messerschmitt Bf 109* is now complete. It is ready for finishing in a natural wood finish, or you can paint the aircraft in authentic colors.

Illus. 29.4   Cut each part to shape on a band saw. Finish shaping by sanding as required on a bench-mounted belt sander.

16. This model can be displayed freestanding, mounted on a desk plaque if the landing gear was installed, or placed on a hardwood stand if you choose to omit the landing gear for display in a flying attitude.

P-38 Lightning   Project 30

Illus. 30.1

The *P-38 Lightning* was built by Lockheed Aircraft Company in 1939 (Illus. 30.1). As its name implies, it was fast, versatile, and effective. This twin engine aircraft worked superbly as a high altitude, long range fighter, the purpose for which it was designed.

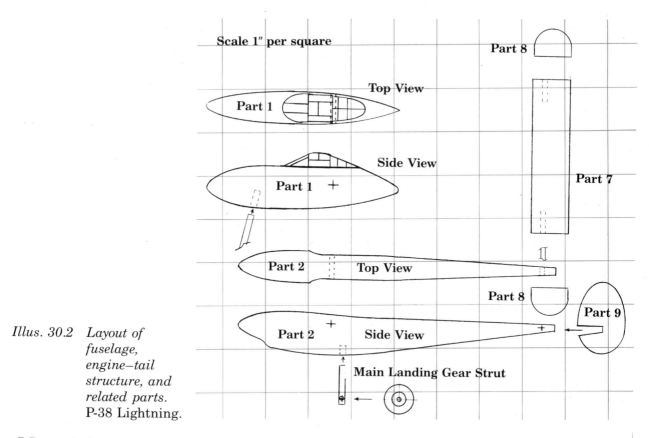

Scale 1″ per square

Top View

Part 1

Side View

Part 1

Part 2   Top View

Part 2   Side View

Main Landing Gear Strut

Part 8

Part 7

Part 8

Part 9

Illus. 30.2   Layout of fuselage, engine–tail structure, and related parts. P-38 Lightning.

Materials List

Hardwood Stock, ¾″ × 4″ × 20″ ...... *1 each*
Hardwood Dowel, ⅛″ diameter .... *15″*
Hardwood Toy Wheels, ¾″ diameter ... *2 each*
Hardwood Toy Wheels, ½″ diameter ... *2 each*
Carpenter's Glue .... *small container*

Cutting List

Part 1 . . . Fuselage .... *Make 1*
Part 2 . . . Engine-Tail Structure ..... *Make 2*
Part 3 . . . Right Outboard Wing ..... *Make 1*
Part 4 . . . Right Inboard Wing ...... *Make 1*
Part 5 . . . Left Inboard Wing .... *Make 1*
Part 6 . . . Left Outboard Wing ...... *Make 1*
Part 7 . . . Horizontal Stabilizer,
middle .... *Make 1*
Part 8 . . . Horizontal Stabilizer, tip ... *Make 2*
Part 9 . . . Vertical Stabilizer .... *Make 2*

Instructions

LAYOUT

1. Lay out Parts 1 through 9 on the ¾″ hardwood stock (Illus. 30.2 and 30.3).

NOTE: Some of the parts do not require the full ¾″ thickness of the stock and must be ripped to the proper thicknesses. The horizontal stabilizer and the vertical stabilizer (Parts 7, 8, and 9) should have a thickness of ³/₁₆″; the thicknesses of the other parts are indicated in Illus. 30.2 and 30.3.

2. Use a band saw or jigsaw to cut all of the above parts to their basic shape.

3. Use a bench-mounted belt sander to form and shape each of these parts to the finished shape required (Illus. 30.4).

ASSEMBLY

4. Mark each of the drilling points on the above parts (Illus. 30.2 and 30.3). All of these holes will be drilled to a diameter of ⁵/₃₂″.

NOTE: Many of the holes are not to be drilled completely through the parts.

5. Drill all of the holes at this time.

6. This model will be assembled by using guide pins made from ⅛″ dowel. The

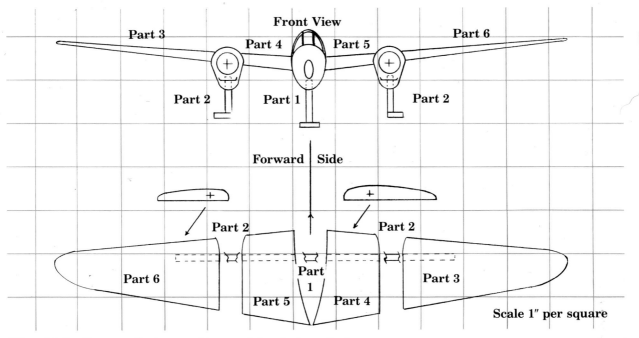

Front View

Part 3   Part 4   Part 5   Part 6

Part 2   Part 1   Part 2

Forward | Side

Part 2   Part 2

Part 6   Part 5   Part 1   Part 4   Part 3

Scale 1″ per square

Illus. 30.3   Layout of wing sections and front view of wing-engine-fuselage assembly. P-38 Lightning.

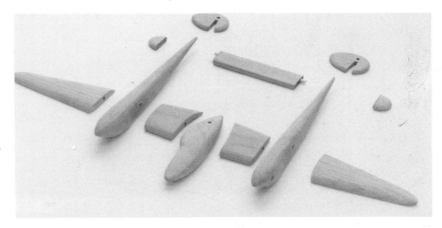

Illus. 30.4   Cut each part to shape on a band saw or jigsaw. Finish shaping by sanding as required on a bench-mounted belt sander.

lengths required will be one 6″ section and two ½″ sections. Cut these pins to length now.

7. The fuselage and engine-tail parts and the four wing parts (Parts 1 through 6) will be assembled in a single operation using the 6″ guide pin.

8. Illus. 30.3 shows the proper configuration of these parts in relation to the 6″ guide pin. Simply glue each part in place along the guide pin, beginning at one end and working towards the other. First try this operation without glue to assure a proper

fit. When the glue is applied, check carefully that each piece is correctly aligned and set the assembly aside until the glue dries.

9. Glue the two ½″ guide pines into the holes in the ends of the middle horizontal stabilizer (Part 7). They should extend by about ⅛″ (Illus. 30.2).

10. Now glue this assembly into place by slightly spreading the tail ends of the two engine-tail structures and slipping the two guide pins into the holes prepared towards the rear (Illus. 30.2). Make sure

the horizontal stabilizer middle is aligned properly with the wing-fuselage-engine assembly.

11. The tips of the horizontal stabilizer (Parts 8) are now simply glued to the outer side of each engine-tail piece (Part 2). Carefully align these so that they appear to be extensions of the middle section of the horizontal stabilizer (Illus. 30.2).

12. Glue the vertical stabilizers (Parts 9) in place by sliding them over the rear end of the engine-tail structures (Parts 2) as shown in Illus. 30.2, side view.

13. If you would prefer displaying your *P-38* in a flying attitude with wheels retracted, you can omit Steps 14 through 17.

14. Cut two main landing gear struts from ⅛" dowel to be ⅞" long. Glue them into the main landing gear mounting holes on the underside of the engine-tail structures (Illus. 30.2).

15. Cut the nose landing gear strut from ⅛" dowel to be 1" long. Glue this into the hole prepared in the underside of the fuselage (Illus. 30.2).

16. The landing gear axles are also cut from ⅛" dowel. The axles for the two main landing gear are ⅜" long and are glued to the main struts as shown in Illus. 30.3, front view. The nose landing gear axle is ½" long and is glued to the nose strut also as shown in Illus. 30.3, front view.

17. Glue two ¾"-diameter hardwood toy wheels to the main landing gear axles and two ½"-diameter hardwood toy wheels to either side of the axle of the nose landing gear.

18. Your *P-38 Lightning* is complete except for finishing (Illus. 30.5). You can preserve the natural wood finish or paint the aircraft in its authentic silver color.

19. To display your *P-38* you will need to mount it on a desk plaque because the solid wood aircraft is not balanced to sit on its tricycle landing gear without support. It may also be displayed in a flying attitude on a hardwood stand.

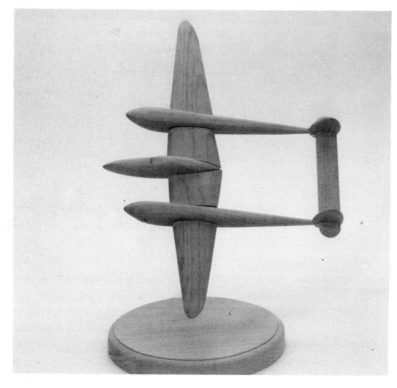

Illus. 30.5 Fully assembled P-38 Lightning *in a flying attitude on a hardwood stand.*

P-39 Airacobra

Illus. 31.1

The *P-39 Airacobra* was built in 1939 by Bell Aircraft Corporation (Illus. 31.1). The design was unique with the engine mounted just behind the pilot in order to place it in the center of gravity over the wing. This idea did not increase performance as was expected. Although the aircraft did well, it was no match for some of its contemporaries.

Materials List

Hardwood Stock, ¾" × 4" × 15" ...... *1 each*
Hardwood Dowel, ⅛" diameter .... *12"*
Hardwood Toy Wheels, ¾ diameter ... *2 each*
Hardwood Toy Wheels, ½" diameter ... *2 each*
Carpenter's Glue .... *small container*

Cutting List

Part 1 ... *Fuselage* .... *Make 1*
Part 2 ... *Right Wing Half* .... *Make 1*
Part 3 ... *Left Wing Half* .... *Make 1*
Part 4 ... *Horizontal Stabilizer Half* *Make 2*
Part 5 ... *Vertical Stabilizer* .... *Make 1*
Part 6 ... *Main Landing Gear Door* *Make 2*

Instructions

LAYOUT

1. Lay out Parts 1 through 6 on the ¾" hardwood stock (Illus. 31.2 and 31.3).
   NOTE: Some of these parts do not require the full ¾" thickness of the stock and must be ripped to the proper thickness. The horizontal stabilizer halves and the vertical stabilizer (Parts 4 and 5) are to be ³⁄₁₆" thick; the thicknesses of the other parts are indicated in Illus. 31.2 and 31.3.
2. Use your band saw to cut these parts to their basic shapes.
3. Use a bench-mounted belt sander to shape the parts (Illus. 31.4).

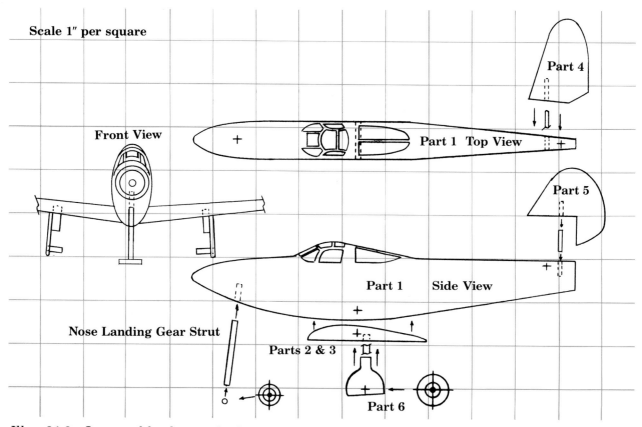

Illus. 31.2 Layout of fuselage and related parts. P-39 Airacobra.

ASSEMBLY

4. Mark all of the drilling points on the above parts (Illus. 31.2 and 31.3). Each of these holes is to be drilled with a ⁵⁄₃₂″ drill bit.
   NOTE: Some of the holes are not to be drilled completely through the parts.

5. Drill all of the holes at this time.

6. The wing halves (Parts 2 and 3), the horizontal stabilizer halves (Parts 4), and the vertical stabilizer (Part 5) will be installed using guide pins. Make these guide pins from ⅛″ dowel sections cut to lengths of 2¼″, 1¼″, and ¾″, respectively.

7. Install the wing halves (Parts 2 and 3) by first inserting the 2¼″ guide pin through the hole prepared in the fuselage. Then press the wing halves onto each end until they butt firmly against the fuselage (Part 1). Use carpenter's glue to secure these parts in place. Align these parts

carefully with respect to the fuselage (Illus. 31.2).

8. Glue the horizontal stabilizer halves (Parts 4) in place in the same way using the 1¼″ guide pin. Position these parts so that they are parallel with the wing and in proper alignment with the fuselage (Illus. 31.2).

9. The vertical stabilizer (Part 5) can now be installed in the same manner using the ¾″ guide pin. Set this part perpendicular to the horizontal stabilizer and parallel with the midline of the fuselage (Illus. 31.2).

10. If you would prefer displaying the *P-39* with the wheels retracted, omit Steps 11 through 16.

11. Cut two main landing gear struts from ⅛″ dowel to a length of ⅝″. Glue these struts into the holes prepared in the underside of the wings (Illus. 31.2).

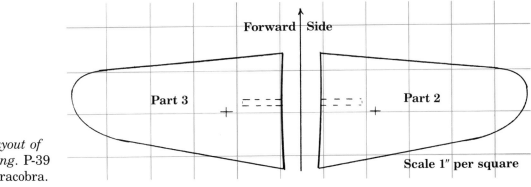

Forward | Side

Part 3

Part 2

Scale 1" per square

Illus. 31.3 Layout of wing. P-39 Airacobra.

12. Cut the main landing gear axles from ⅛" dowel to a length of ⅜", and glue them into the holes in the landing gear doors (Parts 6) as shown in Illus. 31.2, front view.

13. Now glue the landing gear doors (Parts 6) onto the main landing gear struts and butted against the underside of the wings (Illus. 31.2, front view).

14. Cut the nose landing gear strut from ⅛" dowel to a length of 1¼". Glue this strut into the corresponding hole under the nose of the aircraft (Illus. 31.2).

15. Cut a ½" length of ⅛" dowel for the nose landing gear axle. Glue the axle to the bottom of the nose landing gear strut (Illus. 31.2, front view).

16. Glue two ¾"-diameter hardwood toy wheels to the main landing gear axles and two ½"-diameter hardwood toy wheels to the nose landing gear axle.

17. Your *P-39 Airacobra* is complete except for finishing (Illus. 31.5). You can paint the aircraft with authentic colors to add a sense of realism to the display, or you can preserve the natural wood finish to show the qualities of the wood and your workmanship.

18. This solid wood model must be displayed on a desk plaque if it is to stand on its wheels because it will not balance properly on the tricycle landing gear without support. The *P-39 Airacobra* can also be displayed in a flying attitude on a hardwood stand whether the wheels are up or down.

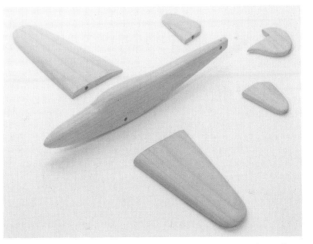

Illus. 31.4 Cut each part to shape on a band saw. Finish shaping by sanding as required on a bench-mounted belt sander.

Illus. 31.5 Fully assembled P-39 Airacobra in a flying attitude on a hardwood stand.

North American Harvard/Texan SNJ

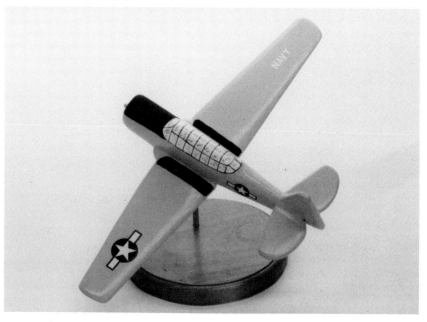

Illus. 32.1

The *North American Harvard/Texan SNJ* trainer was the most widely used aircraft of its day (Illus. 32.1). It could closely simulate actual fighters and dive-bombers for training. The *SNJ* was used in countries all over the world to train pilots for combat.

Materials List

Hardwood Block, 1½″ × 2½″ × 9″ .... 1 each
Hardwood Stock, ¾″ × 4″ × 10″ ...... 1 each
Hardwood Dowel, ¼″ diameter .... 4″
Hardwood Dowel, ³⁄₁₆″ diameter .... 2″
Hardwood Dowel, ⅛″ diameter .... 12″
Carpenter's Glue .... small container

Cutting List

Part 1 ... Fuselage .... Make 1
Part 2 ... Right Wing Half .... Make 1
Part 3 ... Left Wing Half .... Make 1
Part 4 ... Horizontal Stabilizer Half Make 2
Part 5 ... Vertical Stabilizer Half .... Make 1
Part 6 ... Propeller .... Make 1

Instructions

LAYOUT

1. Lay out the fuselage (Part 1) on the hardwood block (Illus. 32.2).
2. Lay out Parts 2 through 5 on the ¾″ hardwood stock (Illus. 32.2 and 32.3).
3. Use a band saw to cut these parts to their basic shapes.
4. Use a bench-mounted belt sander to form and shape each part as required (Illus. 32.4).

ASSEMBLY

5. Mark all of the drilling points on the above parts (Illus. 32.2 and 32.3). These

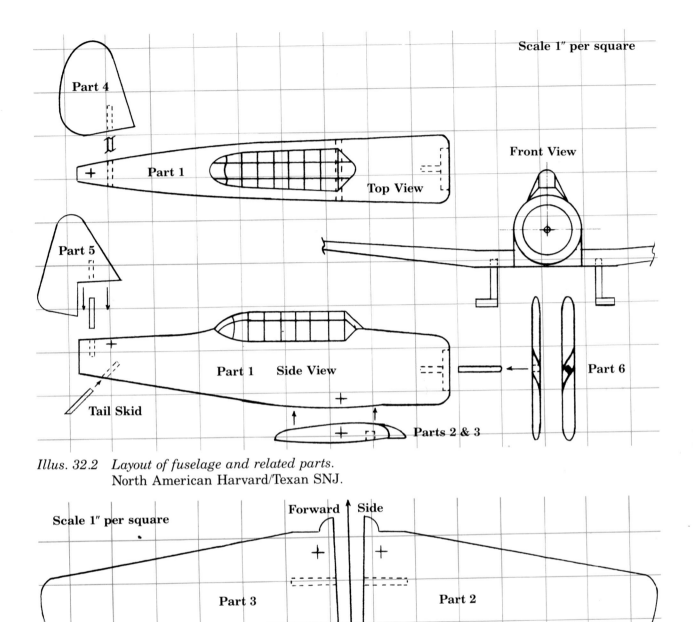

Scale 1″ per square

Part 4

Part 1

Top View

Front View

Part 5

Part 1   Side View

Tail Skid

Parts 2 & 3

Part 6

Illus. 32.2   Layout of fuselage and related parts.
North American Harvard/Texan SNJ.

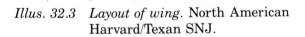

Scale 1″ per square

Forward   Side

Part 3

Part 2

Illus. 32.3   Layout of wing. North American
Harvard/Texan SNJ.

holes are to be a diameter of ⁵⁄₃₂″ with the exception of the propeller drive shaft hole which is to be a ⁷⁄₃₂″ diameter.
NOTE: Some of these holes are not to be drilled completely through the parts.

The engine area is to be counter set with a ⅞″ center bore drill bit to a depth of about ⅛″.

6. Drill all of the holes at this time.
7. The wing halves (Parts 2 and 3), the horizontal stabilizer halves (Parts 4), and the vertical stabilizer (Part 5) are to be installed using guide pins made from ⅛″ dowel cut to lengths of 3″, 1½″, and 1″, respectively.
8. Glue the wing halves (Parts 2 and 3) into

Illus. 32.4   Cut each part to shape on a band saw. Finish shaping by sanding as required on a bench-mounted belt sander.

place by first passing the 3″ guide pin through the hole prepared in the fuselage (Part 1). Then press the wing halves onto it until they butt firmly against the fuselage (Illus. 32.2). Position these parts so that they are properly aligned with respect to the fuselage.

9. The horizontal stabilizer halves (Parts 4) are to be installed in a like manner using the 1½″ guide pin. Align them as one piece to be level with the wing and fuselage (Illus. 32.2).

10. Glue the vertical stabilizer (Part 5) into position using the 1″ guide pin. Set it perpendicular to the horizontal stabilizer and in line with the midline of the fuselage (Illus. 32.2).

11. Cut the propeller drive shaft from ³⁄₁₆″ dowel to a ¾″ length, and glue it into the hole prepared in the nose of the aircraft (Illus. 32.2).

12. Installation of a propeller is optional. If you would prefer displaying this model in a flying attitude, omit the propeller to give the illusion that it is spinning.

13. The propeller is made from ¼″ dowel cut to a 3½″ length following the directions in Step 4 of Project 2 (page 10).

14. If you would like to display the *SNJ* in a flying attitude with the wheels retracted, omit Steps 15 through 18.

15. Cut two landing gear struts from ⅛″ dowel to a length of 1⅛″, and glue them into the holes prepared in the underside of the wing (Illus. 32.2, front view).

16. Make the landing gear axles from two sections of ⅛″ dowel cut to a ⅜″ length. Glue these axles in place at the lower end of the landing gear struts as shown in Illus. 32.2, front view).

17. Attach a ¾″-diameter hardwood toy wheel to each landing gear axle with a drop of glue.

18. Cut a ¾″ section of ⅛″ dowel for the tail skid, and glue it into the prepared mounting hole (Illus. 32.2, side view).

19. Your *North American Harvard/Texan SNJ* is complete except for finishing. You can paint the aircraft in authentic color to add a sense of realism, or you can preserve the natural wood finish to show the qualities of the woods and your workmanship.

20. The *North American Harvard/Texan SNJ* can be displayed freestanding or mounted on a desk plaque or flying stand.

Consolidated Vultee B-24 Liberator

Illus. 33.1

The *B-24 Liberator* was the "aircraft of the future" when it was originally built in 1939 (Illus. 33.1). It had many electrically controlled features including the gun turrets and the landing gear. It was expensive and hard to handle, but more of these aircraft were built than any other in the history of aviation in the United States. The *B-24* bomber was capable of carrying 75 percent of its own weight in payload and it could fly 2200 mi. Another of the truly great large planes, it was used by U.S. forces well into the 1950s.

Materials List

Hardwood Block, 1⅛" × 1½" × 10" . . . 1 each
Hardwood Stock, ¾" × 4" × 8" . . . . 1 each
Hardwood Dowel, ¾" diameter . . . . 10"
Hardwood Dowel, ¼" diameter . . . . 1"
Hardwood Dowel, ⅛" diameter . . . . 12"
Hardwood Screw Buttons, ½" diameter 2 each
Hardwood Toy Wheels, ¾" diameter . . . 4 each
Carpenter's Glue . . . . small container

Cutting List

Part 1 . . . Fuselage . . . . Make 1
Part 2 . . . Right Wing Half . . . . Make 1
Part 3 . . . Left Wing Half . . . . Make 1
Part 4 . . . Horizontal Stabilizer . . . . . . Make 1
Part 5 . . . Vertical Stabilizer . . . . Make 2
Part 6 . . . Outboard Engine Cowling Make 2
Part 7 . . . Inboard Engine Cowling . . Make 2

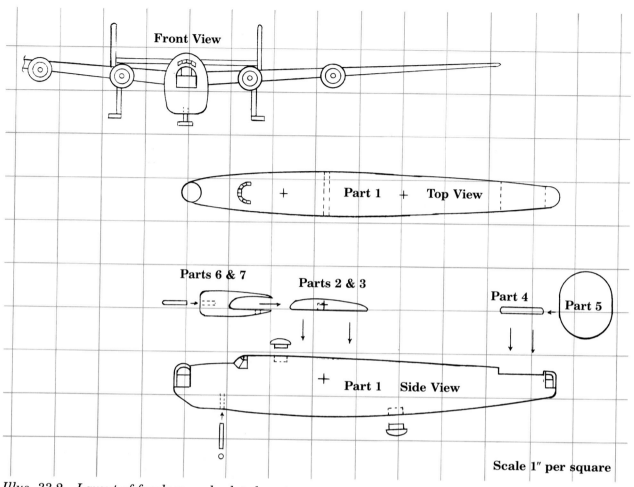

Illus. 33.2   Layout of fuselage and related parts.
Consolidated Vultee B-24 Liberator.

Instructions

LAYOUT

1. Lay out the fuselage (Part 1) on the hardwood block (Illus. 33.2).
2. Lay out Parts 2 through 5 on the ¾" hardwood stock (Illus. 33.2 and 33.3).
   NOTE: These parts do not require the full ¾" thickness and must be ripped to the proper thickness as shown in Illus. 33.2 and 33.3.
3. Lay out Parts 6 and 7 on the ¾"-diameter hardwood dowel (Illus. 33.2 and 33.3).
4. Use a band saw to cut these parts to their basic shapes.
5. Use a bench-mounted belt sander to form and shape each part to its finished shape as required (Illus. 33.4).

ASSEMBLY

6. Mark all of the above parts with the drilling points shown in Illus. 33.2 and 33.3. The holes are to be ⁵⁄₃₂" diameter with exception to the gun turret mounting holes which are ½" diameter.
   NOTE: Some holes are not to be drilled completely through the parts.
7. Cut a 3" guide pin from ⅛" dowel for installing the wing halves.
8. Glue the wing halves (Parts 2 and 3) into place by first passing the guide pin through the hole prepared in the fuselage (Part 1). Then press the wing halves onto it until they butt firmly against the fuselage. Set the wings level with the fu-

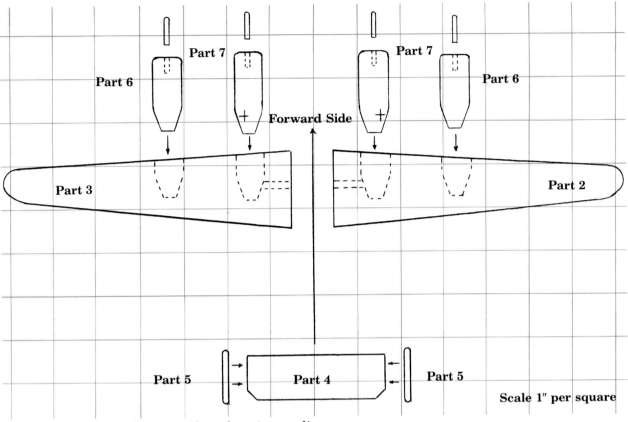

Illus. 33.3 *Layout of wing, tail, and engine cowlings.*
Consolidated Vultee B-24 Liberator.

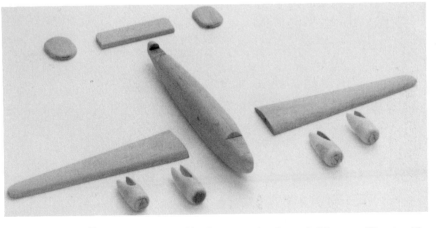

Illus. 33.4 *Cut each part to shape on a band saw. Finish shaping by sanding as required on a bench-mounted belt sander.*

selage and raise the wingtips upwards until they are ¾″ higher than the base of the wing (Illus. 33.2, front view).

9. Glue the horizontal stabilizer (Part 4) in place by positioning it in the notch prepared at the rear of the fuselage (Illus. 33.2). Set it level and perpendicular to the midline of the fuselage.

10. Install the vertical stabilizers (Parts 5) with carpenter's glue and a ⅝″ wire brad for each (Illus. 33.2 and 33.3). Position them properly and assure that they are parallel to one another.

11. Use the two ½″-diameter hardwood screw buttons for gun turrets, and install them into the prepared holes (Illus. 33.2).

12. Glue the four engine cowlings (Parts 6 and 7) into place according to the dashed lines in Illus. 33.3.

 NOTE: The longer cowlings are to be installed as the inboard engines (Illus. 33.2 and 33.3).

13. Make four propeller drive shafts from ⅛" dowel cut to a length of ½". Glue each of them into the holes at the front of the engine cowlings (Illus. 33.2 and 33.3). Make sure that each drive shaft extends uniformly to ¼".

14. If you would prefer displaying the *B-24 Liberator* in a flying attitude with wheels retracted, omit Steps 15 through 20.

15. Make two main landing gear struts from ½" sections of ⅛" dowel. Glue these into the holes on the underside of the inboard engine cowlings (Illus. 33.2).

16. Make the axles for the main landing gear from ⅜" sections of ⅛" dowel. Glue these to the bottom end of the struts as shown in the front view of Illus. 33.2.

17. Glue a ¾"-diameter hardwood toy wheel to each of the main landing gear axles.

18. Cut the nose gear strut from ⅛" dowel to a ⅜" length. Glue it into the nose gear mounting hole on the underside of the forward end of the fuselage (Illus. 33.2).

19. Cut the axle from ⅛" dowel to a 3/16" length. Glue the axle across the strut as shown in the front view of Illus. 33.2.

20. Properly scaled hardwood toy wheels to use for the nose gear wheels are unavailable because of the size of the model. Make wheels from ¼" dowel by cutting two wafers from the dowel only ⅛" thick. Round these parts by sanding so that they better approximate wheels. Glue them to the ends of the nose gear axle.

21. Your *B-24 Liberator* is now complete and ready for finishing (Illus. 33.5). You can preserve the natural wood finish to show the quality of the wood and your workmanship or you can paint the aircraft in authentic colors to add a sense of realism to its display.

22. Display your *B-24* by mounting it on a desk stand to set it up on its tricycle landing gear since its weight distribution is off balance. It may also be displayed in a flying attitude on a hardwood stand.

Illus. 33.5 Fully assembled Consolidated Vultee B-24 Liberator *in a flying attitude on a hardwood stand.*

Spitfire MK IIB

Illus. 34.1

The *Spitfire MK IIB* was a highly maneuverable hard hitting, British-built fighter that was classed with the *P-40* from the United States and the German *Messerschmitt* (Illus. 34.1). The *Spitfire* won fame in the skies over Europe and made its mark in the hands of skilled British pilots as an adversary not to be taken lightly.

Materials List

Hardwood Block, 1½″ × 2″ × 10″ . . . . 1 each
Hardwood Stock, ¾″ × 4″ × 8″ . . . . 1 each
Hardwood Dowel, ¼″ diameter . . . . 3″
Hardwood Dowel, ⅛″ diameter . . . . 10″
Hardwood Toy Wheels, ¾″ diameter . . . 2 each
Carpenter's Glue . . . . small container

Cutting List

Part 1 . . . Fuselage . . . . Make 1
Part 2 . . . Right Wing Half . . . . Make 1
Part 3 . . . Left Wing Half . . . . Make 1
Part 4 . . . Horizontal Stabilizer Half Make 2
Part 5 . . . Vertical Stabilizer . . . . Make 1
Part 6 . . . Landing Gear Door . . . . Make 2

Instructions

LAYOUT

1. Lay out the fuselage (Part 1) on the hardwood block (Illus. 34.2).
2. Lay out Parts 2 through 6 on the ¾″ hardwood stock (Illus. 34.2 and 34.3).
   NOTE: these parts do not require the full ¾″ thickness and must be ripped to the proper thicknesses. The horizontal stabilizer halves and the vertical stabilizer (Parts 4 and 5) are ³⁄₁₆″ thick; other parts have their thickness indicated in Illus. 34.2 and 34.3.
3. Use a band saw to cut these parts to their basic shapes.

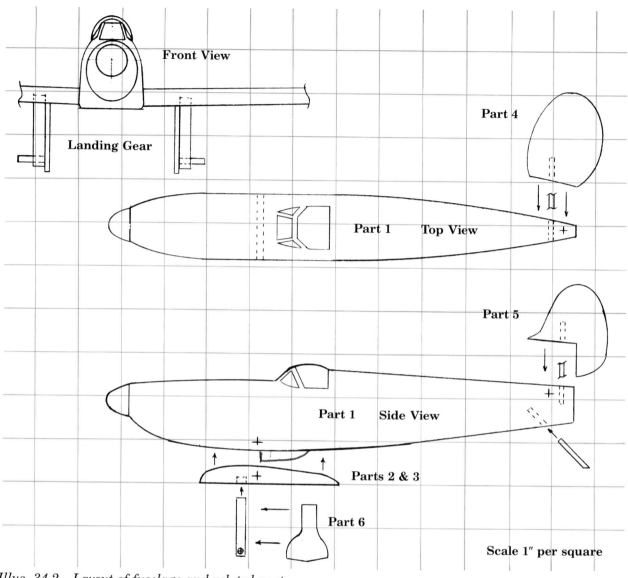

Illus. 34.2   Layout of fuselage and related parts.
Spitfire MK IIB.

4. Use a bench-mounted belt sander to form and shape each of the parts to its finished shape as required (Illus. 34.4).

ASSEMBLY

5. Mark each of the drilling points on the above parts (Illus. 34.2 and 34.3). The landing gear mounting holes on the underside of the wing halves (Parts 2 and 3) are to be drilled to a ⁹/₃₂″ diameter; each of the remaining holes is to be a ⁵/₃₂″ diameter.

NOTE: Some of these holes are not intended to be drilled completely through the parts.

6. Cut a 3″ long guide pin from ⅛″ dowel for mounting the wing halves (Part 2 and 3) to the fuselage (Part 1).

7. Glue the wing halves (Part 2 and 3) in place by first passing the guide pin through the hole prepared in the fuselage (Part 1). Then press the wing halves onto it until they butt firmly against the sides of the fuselage. Align the wings properly

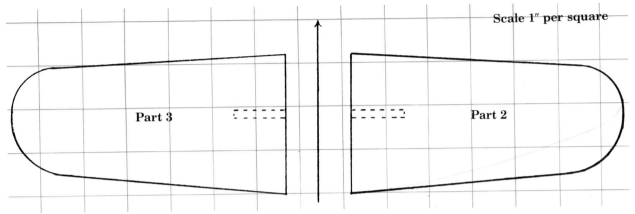

Illus. 34.3   Layout of wing. Spitfire MK IIB.

Part 3

Part 2

Illus. 34.4   Cut each part to shape on a band saw. Finish shaping by sanding as required on a bench-mounted belt sander.

with respect to the fuselage and raise the wingtips upwards until they are ½″ higher than the base of the wing.

8. Install the horizontal stabilizer halves (Parts 4) in the same way by using a 1¼″ guide pin cut from ⅛″ dowel. Set these parts level with respect to the rest of the assembly (Illus. 34.2).

9. A ¾″ guide pin cut from ⅛″ dowel is used to install the vertical stabilizer (Part 5). Set this part perpendicular to the horizontal stabilizer and parallel to the midline of the fuselage (Illus. 34.2).

10. If you would prefer displaying this fighter

aircraft in a flying attitude with the wheels retracted, omit the landing gear installation steps, Steps 11 through 16.

11. Make two landing gear struts from ¼″ dowel cut to lengths of 1¼″. Drill a 5⁄32″-diameter hole a distance of ¼″ from one end (Illus. 34.2).

12. Cut two landing gear axles from ⅛″ dowel to 7⁄16″ lengths. Glue them into the holes drilled in Step 11 as shown in the front view of Illus. 34.2.

13. Glue a ¾″ hardwood toy wheel to each of the axles.

14. Now glue these landing gear assemblies

into the mounting holes on the underside of each wing (Illus. 34.2).

15. Glue the landing gear doors (Parts 6) to the inside of the landing gear struts as shown in the front view of Illus. 34.2.

16. Cut a tail skid from ⅛″ dowel to a ¾″ length. Glue it in place in the hole prepared at the rear of the fuselage.

17. Your *Spitfire* is now complete except for finishing (Illus. 34.5). Finishing can be done with natural wood finishes, or you can paint the aircraft with authentic colors to add a sense of realism to your display.

18. Display the *Spitfire MK IIB* freestanding, mounted on a desk plaque if the landing gear was installed, or in a flying attitude on a hardwood stand if the wheels are retracted.

Illus. 34.5 Fully assembled Spitfire MK IIB *in a flying attitude on a hardwood stand.*

A6M5 Zero-sen

Illus. 35.1

The notorious *Zero* of the Japanese Empire was among those many aircraft that startled the world on the morning of December 7, 1941 at Pearl Harbor (Illus. 35.1). The *A6M5 Zero-sen* was fast and efficient in aerial combat, for which it was designed. This carrier-based aircraft gave the Japanese Navy a far-reaching capability in the Pacific.

Materials List

Hardwood Block, 1⅝″ × 2″ × 9″ . . . . . *1 each*
Hardwood Stock, ¾″ × 4″ × 6″ . . . . *1 each*
Hardwood Dowel, ½″ diameter . . . . *1″*
Hardwood Dowel, ¼″ diameter . . . . *3½″*
Hardwood Dowel, ⅛″ diameter . . . . *12″*
Hardwood Toy Wheels, ¾″ diameter . . . *2 each*
Carpenter's Glue . . . . *small container*

Cutting List

Part 1 . . . Fuselage . . . . *Make 1*
Part 2 . . . Right Wing Half . . . . *Make 1*
Part 3 . . . Left Wing Half . . . . *Make 1*
Part 4 . . . Horizontal Stabilizer Half Make 2
Part 5 . . . Vertical Stabilizer . . . . *Make 1*
Part 6 . . . Landing Gear Door . . . . *Make 2*
Part 7 . . . Propeller . . . . *Make 1*

Instructions

LAYOUT

1. Lay out the fuselage (Part 1) on the hardwood block (Illus. 35.2).
2. Lay out Parts 2 through 6 on the ¾″ hardwood stock (Illus. 35.2 and 35.3).

NOTE: These parts do not require the

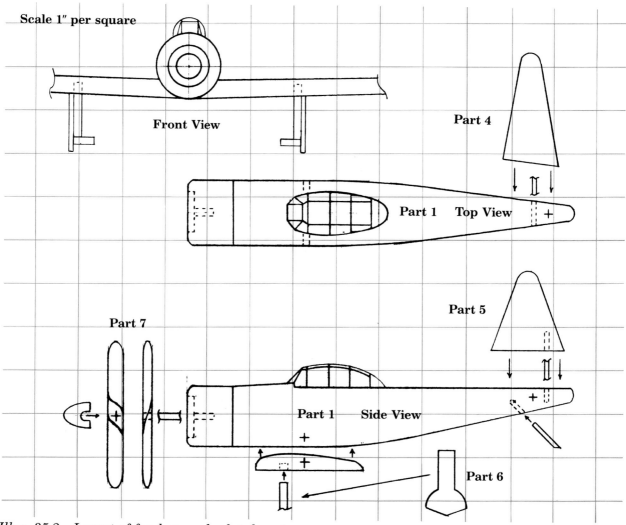

Front View

Part 4

Part 1   Top View

Part 7

Part 5

Part 1   Side View

Part 6

*Illus. 35.2   Layout of fuselage and related parts.
A6M5 Zero-sen.*

full ¾″ thickness and must be ripped to the proper thicknesses as indicated in Illus. 35.2 and 35.3. The horizontal stabilizer halves and the vertical stabilizer (Parts 4 and 5) are to be ³⁄₁₆″ thick; this is not shown in the illustrations.

3. Use a band saw to cut these parts to their basic shapes.

4. Use a bench-mounted belt sander to form and shape the finished shapes as required (Illus. 35.4).

ASSEMBLY

5. Mark each of the drilling points on the above parts (Illus. 35.2 and 35.3). The en-

gine area is to be counter set with a ⅞″ center bore drill to a depth of ⅛″; the remaining holes are to be drilled to a ⁵⁄₃₂″ diameter.

NOTE: some of these holes are not to be drilled completely through the parts.

6. The wing halves (Parts 2 and 3), the horizontal stabilizer halves (Parts 4), and the vertical stabilizer (Part 5) are to be installed using guide pins made from sections of ⅛″ dowel cut to 3″, 2″, and ¾″ lengths, respectively.

7. Glue the wing halves (Parts 2 and 3) in place by first passing the 3″ guide pin through the hole prepared in the side of

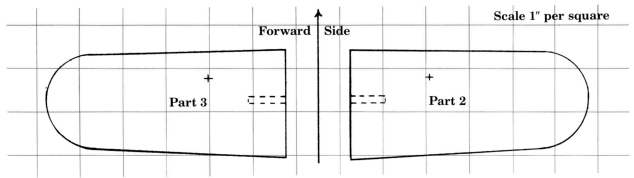

Forward | Side

Part 3

Part 2

Illus. 35.3   Layout of wing. A6M5 Zero-sen.

*Illus. 35.4   Cut each part to
shape on a
band saw.
Finish shaping
by sanding as
required on a
bench-mounted
belt sander.*

the fuselage (Part 1). Then press the wing halves onto either side until they butt firmly against the sides of the fuselage (Illus. 35.2). Position the wings in proper alignment with respect to the fuselage and raise the wingtips upwards until they are about ⅜″ higher than the base of the wing (Illus. 35.2).

8. Install the horizontal stabilizer halves (Parts 4) in the same way using the 2″ guide pin. Set these parts level with respect to the rest of the aircraft (Illus. 35.2).

9. The vertical stabilizer (Part 5) should now be glued into place using the ¾″ guide pin (Illus. 35.2). Position it perpen-

dicular to the horizontal stabilizer and in line with the midline of the fuselage.

10. The propeller (Part 7) is optional. You may prefer to omit it to give the illusion of a spinning propeller. If you choose to install the propeller, make it from ¼″ dowel cut to a length of 3½″. Follow the instructions for making propellers given in Step 4 of Project 2 (page 10).

11. Cut the propeller drive shaft from ⅛″ dowel to a length of ¾″ only if you're planning to install the propeller. Otherwise do not install this drive shaft. If it is to be installed with the propeller, insert it into the hole prepared in the nose of the aircraft (Illus. 35.2).

12. Make the nose spinner, or propeller shaft cover, from ½″ dowel by first shaping the dowel into a rounded cone on your belt sander. Then cut the shaped end ⅝″ from the end (Illus. 35.2). If the propeller was not installed, simply glue this part into the middle of the recessed engine area. If the propeller is in place, the spinner will require a notch to allow it to fit over the propeller (Illus. 35.2, side view). This notch can be made with a ¼″ rat-tail wood rasp.

13. The landing gear is also optional. If you plan to display your *Zero* in a flying, wheels up, attitude, then you may want to omit Steps 14 through 18.

14. Cut two landing gear struts from ⅛″ dowel to a length of 1¼″. Glue these struts into the holes prepared in the underside of the wing.

15. Make two landing gear axles from ⅛″ dowel in lengths of ⅜″. Secure them to the bottom of the struts with carpenter's glue with the axles pointing inwards, as shown in the front view of Illus. 35.2.

16. Install the two ¾″-diameter hardwood toy wheels to the axles.

17. Glue each landing gear door (Part 6) to the outside of each of the landing gear assemblies as shown in Illus. 35.2.

18. Make a ¾″ tail skid from ⅛″ dowel, and glue it in place in the hole prepared at the rear of the fuselage as shown in Illus. 35.2.

19. Your *A6M5 Zero-sen* is now complete and ready for finishing (Illus. 35.5). You can paint the aircraft in authentic colors or preserve the natural wood finish.

20. Display the *Zero* either freestanding, mounted on a desk plaque or in a flying attitude on a hardwood stand if the wheels are up.

Illus. 35.5 Fully assembled A6M5 Zero-sen in a flying attitude on a hardwood stand.

·9·
CLASSIC AIRCRAFT IN AVIATION'S POST-WAR FUTURE

In surveying the vintage aircraft of the world, we have explored flight from its beginnings up to the years immediately prior to World War II. It is true that many of the later aircraft—especially in Chapter 8—were involved extensively in World War II, but their development was in the years before the war. These are all magnificent machines that have taken their place in history—each had a part in the ongoing advancement of aviation.

The aircraft depicted in the following few pages are classics in their own right. They are not the state-of-the-art computer-operated tactical fighting machines of today, yet they are the stepping-stones from the earlier eras to a future typified by jet aircraft and supersonic airspeeds. Developed a little over a half dozen years after the end of the war, these two aircrafts represent the rapidly changing world of aviation.

F-100 Supersabre

Project 36

Illus. 36.1

The *F-100 Supersabre* (Illus. 36.1) was built by North American Aircraft in 1953 as a successor to their earlier *F-86 Sabre*. It was strong and fast, capable in level flight of speeds faster than the speed of sound. This supersonic aircraft became one of the U.S. Air Force's most popular fighters and remained so until well into the 1960s.

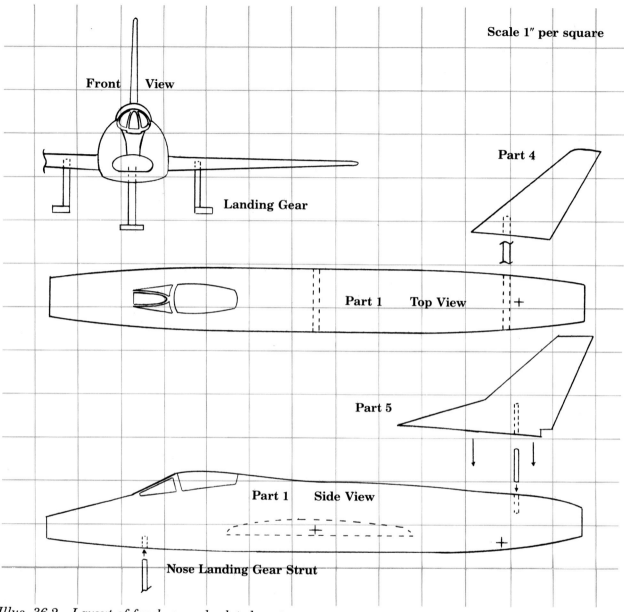

Illus. 36.2   Layout of fuselage and related parts.
F-100 Supersabre.

Materials List

Hardwood Block, 1½″ × 2″ × 14″ ....1 each
Hardwood Stock, ¾″ × 4″ × 12″ ......1 each
Hardwood Dowel, ⅛″ diameter ....12″
Hardwood Toy Wheels, ¾″ diameter ...2 each
Hardwood Toy Wheels, ½″ diameter ...2 each
Carpenter's Glue ....small container

Cutting List

Part 1 . . . Fuselage ....Make 1
Part 2 . . . Right Wing Half ....Make 1

Part 3 . . . Left Wing Half ....Make 1
Part 4 . . . Horizontal Stabilizer Half Make 2
Part 5 . . . Vertical Stabilizer ....Make 1

Instructions

LAYOUT

1. Lay out the fuselage (Part 1) on the hard-wood block (Illus. 36.2).
2. Lay out Parts 2 through 5 on the ¾″ hard-wood stock (Illus. 36.2 and 36.3).

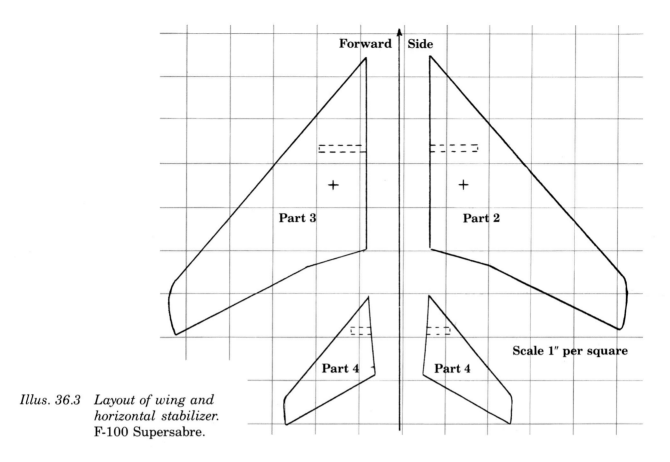

Illus. 36.3 *Layout of wing and horizontal stabilizer. F-100 Supersabre.*

NOTE: These parts do not require the full ¾″ thickness and must be ripped to the proper thicknesses. The horizontal stabilizer halves and the vertical stabilizer (Parts 4 and 5) are to be finished at ³⁄₁₆″; the thicknesses of other parts are shown in Illus. 36.2 and 36.3.

3. Use your band saw to cut these parts to their basic shapes.

4. Use a bench-mounted belt sander to form and shape the parts as required (Illus. 36.4).

ASSEMBLY

5. Mark all of the drilling points on these parts (Illus. 36.2 and 36.3). All of the holes are to be drilled to a ⁵⁄₃₂″ diameter. **NOTE:** Some of these holes are not to be drilled completely through the parts.

6. Drill all of the holes at this time.

7. The installation of the wing halves (Parts 2 and 3), the horizontal stabilizer halves (Parts 4), and the vertical stabilizer (Part 5) will be done using guide pins made from ⅛″ dowel cut to lengths of 3″, 2″, and 1″, respectively.

8. Glue the wing halves (Parts 2 and 3) in place by first inserting the 3″ guide pin through the hole prepared in the side of the fuselage (Part 1). Then press the wing halves onto the guide pin until they butt firmly against the sides of the fuselage. Align the wings so that they are parallel with the midline of the fuselage.

9. Install the horizontal stabilizer halves (Parts 4) in the same manner using the 2″ guide in. Set these parts level with the fuselage and parallel with the wings.

10. The vertical stabilizer (Part 5) is to be installed using the 1″ guide pin. Set this part perpendicular to the horizontal stabilizer and parallel to the midline of the fuselage.

11. If you would prefer displaying the *F-100*

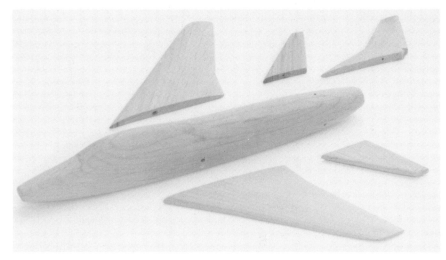

Illus. 36.4 *Cut each part to shape on a band saw. Finish shaping by sanding as required on a bench-mounted belt sander.*

Supersabre in a flying attitude with the wheels up, omit Steps 12 through 17.

12. Make the main landing gear struts from ⅛″ dowel cut to 1″ lengths. Glue these into the holes prepared in the underside of the wings.
13. Cut the main landing gear axles from ⅛″ dowel to a length of ⅜″. Glue these to the lower end of the struts as shown in the front view of Illus. 36.2.
14. Make a nose landing gear strut from ⅛″ dowel cut to a 1¼″ length. Glue it into the hole prepared on the underside of the forward fuselage (Illus. 36.2).
15. Cut ⅛″ dowel to a ½″ length for the nose landing gear axle. Glue it to the lower end

of the nose gear strut as shown in Illus. 36.2, front view.

16. Glue the ¾″-diameter hardwood toy wheels to the main landing gear axles.
17. Glue the ½″-diameter hardwood toy wheels to the nose gear axle.
18. Your *F-100 Supersabre* is now complete and ready for finishing (Illus. 36.5). You can preserve the natural wood finish or paint the aircraft in authentic colors to add a sense of realism.
19. Display this model by simply standing it on its landing gear or mounting it on a desk plaque. If you omitted the landing gear steps, then display the aircraft in a flying attitude on a hardwood stand.

Illus. 36.5 *Fully assembled F-100* Supersabre *in a flying attitude on a hardwood stand.*

F-104 Starfighter

Illus. 37.1

The *Starfighter* is an impressive looking fighter plane (Illus. 37.1). Capable of speeds of more than twice the speed of sound (Mach 2), it can also climb at a rate of 50,000 feet per minute. This jet airplane, built by Lockheed Aircraft in 1954, is an example of the extraordinary advancements in aviation since the early days when man first went aloft in balloons or the first flying machine changed the course of history by staying airborne for less than a dozen seconds. Surely man soars with the eagles on wings of his own.

Materials List
Hardwood Block, 1¾″ × 2¼″ × 16″ . . . 1 each
Hardwood Stock, ¾″ × 4″ × 8″ . . . . 1 each
Hardwood Dowel, ⅛″ diameter . . . . 10″
Hardwood Toy Wheels, ¾″ diameter . . . 2 each
Hardwood Toy Wheels, ½″ diameter . . . 2 each
Carpenter's Glue . . . . small container

Cutting List
Part 1 . . . Fuselage . . . . Make 1
Part 2 . . . Right Wing Half . . . . Make 1
Part 3 . . . Left Wing Half . . . . Make 1
Part 4 . . . Horizontal Stabilizer Half Make 2
Part 5 . . . Vertical Stabilizer . . . . Make 1

Instructions

LAYOUT
1. Lay out the fuselage (Part 1) on the hardwood block (Illus. 37.2).
2. Lay out Parts 2 through 5 on the ¾″ hardwood stock (Illus. 37.2).

NOTE: These parts do not require the full ¾″ thickness and must be ripped to the proper thicknesses. Each of these parts should be ripped to a ³⁄₁₆″ thickness.
3. Use your band saw or jigsaw to cut each part to its basic shape.
4. Use a bench-mounted belt sander to form and shape the parts as required (Illus. 37.3).

ASSEMBLY
5. Mark the drilling points on the parts (Illus. 37.2). Each of the holes is to be drilled to a ⁵⁄₃₂″ diameter.
NOTE: Some of the holes are not to be drilled completely through the parts.
6. Installation of the wing halves (Parts 2 and 3), the horizontal stabilizer halves (Parts 4), and the vertical stabilizer (Part 5) will be done using four 1″ guide pins made from ⅛″ dowel (Illus. 37.2).

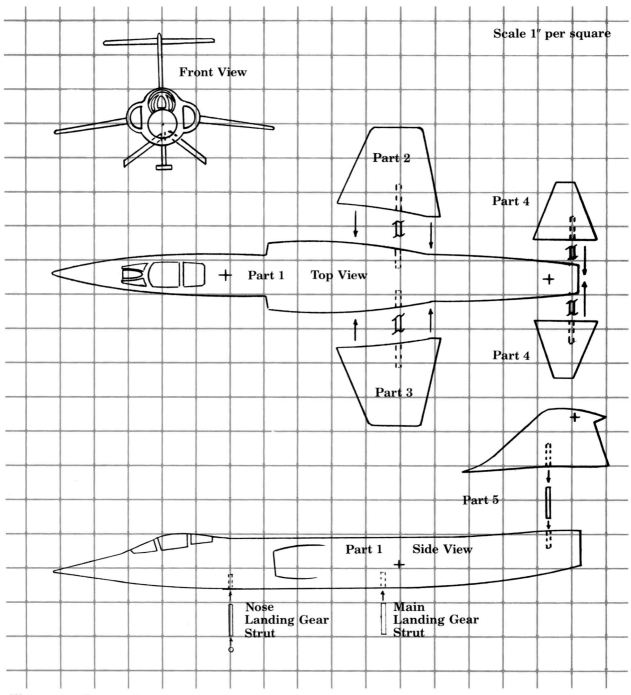

Illus. 37.2   Layout. F-104 Starfighter.

7. Glue each wing half in place by inserting a 1″ guide pin into the hole in the end of the wing half and then pressing it into the hole prepared in the side of the fuselage (Illus. 37.2).

8. Install the vertical stabilizer (Part 5) using a 1″ guide pin pressed into the hole prepared in the top rear of the fuselage (Illus. 37.2).

9. Install the horizontal stabilizer halves (Parts 4) by passing a 1″ guide pin through the hole prepared in the vertical

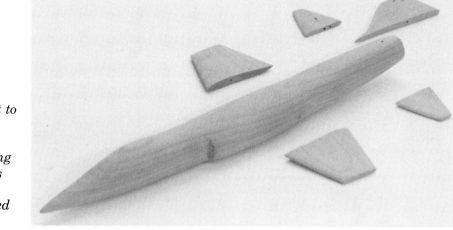

Illus. 37.3   Cut each part to shape on a band saw. Finish shaping by sanding as required on a bench-mounted belt sander.

stabilizer. Press the halves onto the pin until they butt firmly against the vertical stabilizer. Set these parts level with the rest of the project.

10. If you would prefer displaying the *F-104* in a flying attitude with the wheels retracted, omit Steps 11 through 15.

11. Make the main landing gear struts from ⅛″ dowel cut to 1¼″ lengths. Glue these into the prepared holes (Illus. 37.2). Sand the ends of these struts so that the finished face is in a vertical plane with respect to the rest of the project as shown in the front view of Illus. 37.2.

12. Make the nose landing gear strut from ⅛″ dowel cut to a ½″ length. Glue it into the nose gear mounting hole (Illus. 37.2).

13. Make a nose landing gear axle from ⅛″ dowel cut to a length of ½″. Glue it to the lower end of the nose landing gear strut (Illus. 37.2, front view).

14. Glue the two ¾″-diameter hardwood toy wheels to the flat face of the main gear struts. Insert a ³⁄₁₆″ length of ⅛″ dowel into both wheel axle holes as filler.

15. Glue the ½″-diameter hardwood toy wheels to either side of the nose landing gear axle.

16. Your *F-104 Starfighter* is now complete except for finishing (Illus. 37.4). You can preserve the natural wood finish or paint the aircraft in authentic colors.

17. Display your *F-104* by simply placing it on its landing gear freestanding or mounting it on a desk plaque. You can also place the aircraft in a flying attitude on a hardwood stand if the landing gear has been omitted.

Illus. 37.4   Fully assembled F-104 Starfighter in a flying attitude on a hardwood stand.

Metric Conversion

MM—MILLIMETRES   CM—CENTIMETRES

INCHES TO MILLIMETRES AND CENTIMETRES

INCHES	MM	CM	INCHES	CM	INCHES	CM
⅛	3	0.3	9	22.9	30	76.2
¼	6	0.6	10	25.4	31	78.7
⅜	10	1.0	11	27.9	32	81.3
½	13	1.3	12	30.5	33	83.8
⅝	16	1.6	13	33.0	34	86.4
¾	19	1.9	14	35.6	35	88.9
⅞	22	2.2	15	38.1	36	91.4
1	25	2.5	16	40.6	37	94.0
1¼	32	3.2	17	43.2	38	96.5
1½	38	3.8	18	45.7	39	99.1
1¾	44	4.4	19	48.3	40	101.6
2	51	5.1	20	50.8	41	104.1
2½	64	6.4	21	53.3	42	106.7
3	76	7.6	22	55.9	43	109.2
3½	89	8.9	23	58.4	44	111.8
4	102	10.2	24	61.0	45	114.3
4½	114	11.4	25	63.5	46	116.8
5	127	12.7	26	66.0	47	119.4
6	152	15.2	27	68.6	48	121.9
7	178	17.8	28	71.1	49	124.5
8	203	20.3	29	73.7	50	127.0

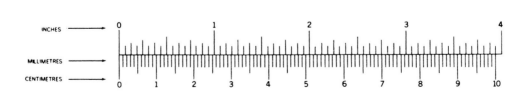

Index